Artistic Pedagogical Technologies
A Primer for Educators

Katherine J. Janzen
Mount Royal University, Canada

Beth Perry
Athabasca University, Canada

Margaret J.A. Edwards
Athabasca University, Canada

Series in Education
VERNON PRESS

Copyright © 2019 Vernon Press, an imprint of Vernon Art and Science Inc, on behalf of the author.

All rights reserved. No part of this publication may be reproduced, stored in a retrieval system, or transmitted in any form or by any means, electronic, mechanical, photocopying, recording, or otherwise, without the prior permission of Vernon Art and Science Inc.

www.vernonpress.com

In the Americas:
Vernon Press
1000 N West Street,
Suite 1200, Wilmington,
Delaware 19801
United States

In the rest of the world:
Vernon Press
C/Sancti Espiritu 17,
Malaga, 29006
Spain

Series in Education

Library of Congress Control Number: 2018964327

ISBN: 978-1-62273-662-1

Hardback: 978-1-62273-533-4

E-book: 978-1-62273-575-4

Product and company names mentioned in this work are the trademarks of their respective owners. While every care has been taken in preparing this work, neither the authors nor Vernon Art and Science Inc. may be held responsible for any loss or damage caused or alleged to be caused directly or indirectly by the information contained in it.

Every effort has been made to trace all copyright holders, but if any have been inadvertently overlooked the publisher will be pleased to include any necessary credits in any subsequent reprint or edition.

Cover design by Vernon Press using elements designed by jcomp / Freepik.

Table of Contents

Foreword by Sharon L. Moore — v

Introduction — ix

Chapter 1   **Artistic Pedagogical Technologies: Beginnings and Evolutions** — 1

Chapter 2   **Theoretical Foundations: The Quantum Perspective of Learning** — 9

Chapter 3   **The Value of Creativity: Technology, Edutainment, and Play in the Classroom** — 31

Chapter 4   **Artistic Pedagogical Technologies: 35 Examples** — 49

Chapter 5   **The Evidence Base: Past, Present and Future** — 75

Chapter 6   **Trying Something New: Motivating Educators to Give APTs a Try** — 115

Chapter 7   **Selected Lesson Plans** — 129

Index — 145

Foreword
by Sharon L. Moore

> "Education is not the filling of a pail, but the lighting of a fire"
> (Yeats, n.d.)

As teachers in post-secondary educational environments, we all hope to inspire the students we teach, to know that somehow we can make a difference in their lives and light a fire and a passion for learning that will continue across their lifespans. Several years ago, I was inspired by the words of Parker Palmer, internationally renowned educator and author, in his book *The Courage to Teach* when he said "when my students and I discover uncharted territory to explore, when the pathway out of a thicket opens up before us, when our experience is illumined by the lightening-life of the mind—then teaching is the finest work I know" (Palmer, 2007, p. 1).

Maybe you have experienced moments like these as an educator. I know that I have and it is at those times when I might think that I have "made it" in my calling. Of course, there are many other moments, but these Parker Palmer moments are the ones that inspire us as educators. They propel us to keep trying to improve our practice of teaching when we see students excited about their learning, and when we see students transformed by their learning.

In *Artistic Pedagogical Technologies*, also known as APTs, authors Janzen, Perry and Edwards offer college and university educators a toolkit of strategies to engage learners in exciting and collaborative learning environments. Born out of their experiences as nurse educators in both traditional face to face, and online teaching and learning environments, they summon us into their classrooms to take a glimpse at innovative activities they have created. These activities invite students into welcoming learning environments and engage them in communities of learning where even students who are studying on their own, such as on an online environment, feel welcomed and part of that community. While the authors describe APTs used in nursing education, this is simply because these are their own teaching environments. The potential applicability of APTs extends to far broader educational contexts and a variety of disciplines.

Through their descriptions of creative arts-based activities, and a discussion of student responses to those activities, we readily see the potential for transformative learning that APTs can have when carried out in classrooms with intention and purpose. We are also reminded of the important role that teachers play in facilitating environments in which this transformation occurs. APTs have the ability to engage both teachers and learners and to help teachers become more real, particularly in online educational environments. Through thoughtful and judicious use, APTs can facilitate the felt social presence of the teacher. Parker Palmer said:

> TEACHING MATTERS and that good teachers possess a capacity for connectedness. They are able to weave a complex web of connections among themselves, their subjects, and their students so that students can learn to weave a world for themselves. The methods used vary widely.... The connections made by the teachers are not held in their method, but in their hearts– meaning *heart* in the strictest sense, as the place where intellect and emotion and spirit and will converge in the human self. (2007, p. 11)

This quote is very apropos to what the authors suggest about how APTs can be viewed as "soul work" where "APTs call to the soul and manifest that which is deep within each of us" (Janzen, Perry, Edwards, 2019, p. 2).

Over the past decade, there has been a growing recognition of the important role that arts-based initiatives can play in education, health care and research. In 2018, *The Journal of Cultural and Pedagogical Inquiry* published a special issue on Creating a Canvas: Artistic Pedagogies in Academia. In addition to the research of the authors of *Artistic Pedagogical Technologies*, other arts-based initiatives have focused on research (Leavy, 2015), health (McNiff, 2004), elementary education (Steckel, Harlow Shinas, & Van Vaerenewyck, 2015) and future technology (Kurach, 2016) to mention only a few.

Clearly, *Artistic Pedagogical Technologies* is leading the way as a primer for educators who are willing to use APTs in the classroom. More than just a list of "how to" strategies, however, Janzen, Perry and Edwards, contextualize these strategies within an educational theoretical framework that grounds APTs within the quantum theory of learning. From "humble beginnings" as Dr. Perry describes, the use of APTs has been researched for the past 15 years in both graduate and undergraduate nursing programs. Students' comments have reinforced the value of these strategies which are clearly outlined in this textbook. In this book, APTs are offered freely for educators to use or adapt for use in their classrooms.

Perhaps the most effective way to summarize the potential for the use of APTs is in the words of one of my own students when we had finished a semester in a graduate course in Advanced Qualitative Research. During the semester, I had incorporated the use of photography (photovoice) and metaphor while teaching about the landscape of qualitative research. I had likened learning about the landscape of qualitative research to various aspects of climbing a mountain and we discussed how essential it is to examine the landscape from various viewpoints. My student, Ruth, shared her experience of that semester as follows:

> "This has been a transformative semester like nothing I could ever have imagined".

This quote by Pema Chodron captures it nicely:

> "The next time there's no ground to stand on, don't consider it an obstacle. Consider it a remarkable stroke of luck. We have no ground to stand on, and at the same time it could soften us and inspire us. We can either cling to security, or we can let ourselves feel exposed, as if we had just been born, as if we had just popped out into the brightness of life and were completely naked... Right there in that inadequate, restless feeling is our wisdom mind".

Ruth went on to say:

> I am learning to read, listen, and look deeply, while letting go of the security of preconceived structures and premature conclusions. I am learning to continually question everything and to trust the emergent processes of understanding. I am learning that I know very little, and can trust myself far more than I dreamed possible. Finally, I am learning that it is a marvelous thing to have good company on the journey – learning from those who have already climbed a little further and reaching out a hand to those scrambling over the rise just below, sharing our trail mix as we marvel at the view and discuss maps and strategies that help us along the way.

As I re-read Ruth's words, I remember that this was truly one of those inspiring moments that I mentioned at the beginning of my comments.

I encourage you to read and engage with the APTs presented in this book. They have been developed, tried and tested by the authors Janzen, Perry and Edwards, who are also exemplary teachers and researchers. Try them out. Adapt them for use in your own classrooms. As a teacher who has taught in distance and online environments for almost forty years, I speak from experience when I say that APTs can transform your teaching and help you to feel more real and engaged with the students in the classroom.

Parker Palmer in his latest book referred to his friend's description of her 16 month old daughter learning to paint. This friend's opening line of an essay was "she's on the brink of everything." Palmer went on to say 'that's exactly where I am today at age seventy-nine. I'm frequently awestruck as I stand on the brink of the rest of my life" (Palmer, 2019, p. 13). When you venture to try something new, like incorporating APTs into your classroom, it can feel like you are 'on the brink of' something new, exciting and transformational in your teaching. It can be a little scary, but the rewards are oh so awesome!

Sharon L. Moore, PhD, RN, R. Psych.
Professor, Athabasca University
Athabasca, Alberta Canada

References

Kurach, M. (2016). The development of future technology teachers' artistic-projective abilities: Foreign experience. *Comparative Professional Pedagogy, 6*(1), 28–35. Retrieved from http://0-search.ebscohost.com.aupac.lib.athabascau.ca/login.aspx?direct=true&db=eric&AN=EJ1124725&site=eds-live

Leavy, P. (2015) *Method meets art: Arts-based research practice (2nd ed.).* New York: Guilford Press.

Palmer, P.J. (2007). T*he courage to teach: Exploring the inner landscape of a teacher's life,* San Francisco, Jossey-Bass.

Palmer, P.J. (2018). *On the brink of everything: Grace, gravity & getting old.* Oakland, CA: Berrett-Koehler Publishers.

Steckel, B., Harlow Shinas, V., & Van Vaerenewyck, L. (2015). Artistic technology integration: Stories from primary and elementary classrooms. *The Reading Teacher, 69*(1), 41-49. DOI:10.1002/trtr.1356. Retrieved from: http://0-eds.a.ebscohost.com.aupac.lib.athabascau.ca/eds/pdfviewer/pdfviewer?vid=4&sid=7bbb8f8f-f603-42d9-971d-98bbebaaaeef%40sessionmgr4008

Yeats, W.B. (n.d.). Retrieved from: https://everydaypowerblog.com/quotes-about-education/

Introduction

Today's educators are resilient. In the face of technological developments that are moving at an almost unbelievable pace, educators are called upon to be tech-savvy to keep up with their students (Alexander, Becker, Cummins & Giesinger, 2017). As each year passes being tech-savvy could be seen as quickly becoming a must (Sterrett & Richardson, 2017). With this, there are many decisions to be made—and not all of them are easy. In particular, "today's [educators] must make tough decisions on how to spend their classroom time. Clear alignment of educational objectives with local, state, and national standards is a necessity. Like the pieces of a huge puzzle, everything must fit properly." (Foreman, 2005, p. 4). However, within the puzzle pieces there remain elements of choice. One of the puzzle pieces can be conceptualized as the delivery of course materials. Within that puzzle piece there exists a myriad of choices. There exists much literature about techniques and interventions to try in the classroom (Abrami, Bernard, Borokhovski, Waddington, Wade, & Persson, 2015; Hultquist & Bradshaw, 2016; Shaffer & Thomas-Brown, 2015). Creativity, especially the use of the creative arts, can infuse a classroom with wonder.

Such is the use of Artistic Pedagogical Technologies or APTs for short. As a collection of creative arts-based strategies, APTs have been researched for 13 years. They have been thoughtfully chosen and tested with much success in the student population. This book is the culmination of that research. From humble beginnings of a single APT to now a collection of 35, APTs show great results in connecting with students.

The use of APTs could be described as soul work (Ashby, 2011; Dirkx, 2001). APTs call to the soul and manifest that which is deep within each of us. APTs, in turn, stir the soul to action and the results can be breathtaking. Although Brown (2018) was talking about poetry, APTs can have a similar effect where APTs "translate emotions to a concrete language that demonstrates the complex and subtle realities of the human soul" (p.1).

While the focus of the examples in the book is on nurse educators because that is our background and experience, we anticipate that APTs can be used effectively (and without much, if any, adaptation) in teaching students from many disciplines. If you teach other health care professionals like pharmacists, rehabilitation therapists, dieticians, or social workers, this book will provide you with valuable instructional strategies. Perhaps you teach teachers, why not give APTs a try in your classes? In turn, the learners you teach may be motivated to use APTs in their classes furthering the effects of these engaging approaches. Even students in fields that seem more number and fact focused (and perhaps less human-focused) such as science or mathematics may find value in engaging in APTs in order to enhance their creativity and help develop a sense of community in their classrooms. Further, APTs can be used in face-to-face, online, and blended classrooms with equal positive benefits. In our view, APTs have potential value for all learners.

The conception of this book came about because of a request from Dr. Carolina Sanchez from Vernon Press that perhaps we share some of our research. Writing this book has been a yearlong venture that has been exciting for us. We hope you enjoy it. Most of all we hope that you try APTs in your classroom and see, as we have seen, wonderful connections with your students, and minds that are expanded due to the use of the creative arts. Like Resnick (2004), "our ultimate goal is a world full of playfully creative [students], who are constantly inventing new opportunities for themselves and their communities" (p. 4).

This community includes educational spaces where educators have the continuous ability to explore, play, and grow. Come along with us and begin a journey as you read this book. This journey is highlighted by creativity and creative processes. We know the best is yet to come. Shall we begin?

References

Abrami, P. C., Bernard, R. M., Borokhovski, E., Waddington, D. I., Wade, C. A., & Persson, T. (2015). Strategies for teaching students to think critically: A meta-analysis. *Review of Educational Research, 85*(2), 275-314.

Alexander, B., Becker, S. A., Cummins, M., & Giesinger, C. H. (2017). *Digital literacy in higher education, Part II: An NMC Horizon project strategic brief* (pp. 1-37). Washington D.C.: The New Media Consortium.

Ashby, S. F. (2011). Soul work: A phenomenological study of college English professors (Order No. 3473529). Available from ProQuest Dissertations & Theses Global.

Bradshaw, M.J., & Hultquist, B. L. (2016). *Innovative teaching strategies in nursing and related health professions.* Burlington, MA: Jones & Bartlett.

Brown, T. (2018). How does poetry communicate feelings and emotions? Retrieved from https://englishsummary.com/poetry-communicate-feelings-emotions/

Dirkx, J. M. (2001). Images, transformative learning and the work of soul. *Adult Learning, 12*(3), 15-16.

Foreman, M. (2005). Bloom's taxonomy: Original and revised. *Emerging Perspectives on Teaching, Learning, and Technology 41*, 47-57. Retrieved from https://www.d41.org/cms/lib/IL01904672/Centricity/Domain/422/BloomsTaxonomy.pdf

Hultquist, B. L & Bradshaw, M. J. (2016). *Innovative teaching strategies in nursing and related health professions.* Burlington, MA: Jones & Bartlett.

Resnick, M. (2004). Edutainment? No thanks. I prefer playful learning. *Associazione Civita Report on Edutainment, 14*, 1-4.

Shaffer, L., & Thomas-Brown, K. (2015). Enhancing teacher competency through co-teaching and embedded professional development. *Journal of Education and Training Studies, 3*(3), 117-125.

Sterrett, W. L., & Richardson, J. W. (2017). Cultivating innovation in an age of accountability: Tech-savvy leadership. *Journal of Cases in Educational Leadership, 20*(4), 27-4

Chapter 1

Artistic Pedagogical Technologies: Beginnings and Evolutions

Beth Perry

The Impetus: Wanting to Feel Less Distant

Artistic Pedagogical Technologies (APTs) had very humble beginnings. I was new to teaching online and at times I felt a disconnect from the students. I was at my home office and they were scattered around the globe in their own learning spaces. How could I let the students know that I was a real person who really cared about them and their learning? My prior teaching had been in face-to-face classrooms where I used a wide variety of learning activities to catch the students' attention and pique their interest in the topic of the class. I pushed them to be creative and used games, puzzles, stories, music, competitions, debates, and other strategies to get and keep their attention.

Students often commented on my instructor evaluations that they loved coming to class because they "never knew what I was going to have them do next." I got the message from this feedback that learners appreciated the new, novel, and unexpected in lesson plans and that a bond between student and teacher (and among class colleagues) could be fostered when learners were asked to participate in learning activities that were different from what they experienced in most other classes. I came to understand that some of these seemingly light-hearted and even frivolous activities resulted in building a sense of class solidarity, fueled positive interpersonal relationships in the group, and importantly led to deep and meaningful discussions and understandings of complex issues and topic.

Bringing my positive experiences in the face-to-face classroom to the online teaching world, I tried to think of ways I could use some of the same learning activities when students were geographically distant from me and one another. My questions to myself were, Could I recreate the positive relationship and learning outcomes with online students? and Would a modified version of some of these unorthodox learning activities be successful with distance education? It took a little resourcefulness and some trial and error, but eventually I managed to reimagine and adapt many of these creative instructional activities so they worked well with online learners. Students seemed excited about trying these unconventional strategies and participation rates, depth of critique and sharing, and a sense of fun and community began to emerge in my online learning spaces. I no longer felt a disconnect from my online students as we engaged together in a variety of instructional activities that brought color, creativity, challenge, competition, and humor to the courses.

Establishing a Research Foundation: The Exemplary Educators Study

About the same time, I started a program of research in 2005 with my faculty colleague Dr. Margaret Edwards. We received funding to do a small research study on what makes some online nurse educators exemplary. My doctoral research completed a few years earlier focused on exemplary clinical nurses so it seemed logical now that I was a nurse educator that I should study what makes some educators outstanding. Given that I was working in the online world, in a faculty of health disciplines, the focus of the study was online nurse educators.

The initial spark for the exemplary online educators' study occurred when we made the very ordinary observation that some of the instructors who taught graduate courses online in our faculty were more successful than others. We began to study strategies used by these outstanding online educators. In part, this initial study concluded that exemplary online educators stimulate interaction and cultivate social presence in the classes they teach. We used the UNESCO definition of interaction (in an online educational context) as learner-course content, learner-learner, or learner-learner exchanges (2012). Social presence was considered "the ability of learners to project their personal characteristics into the community of inquiry, thereby presenting themselves as 'real people'" (Rourke, Anderson & Garrison, 2001, p. 51). Kant (2012) was one of the first researchers to note that social presence is achieved in part through the incorporation of interactive teaching strategies in teaching. Putting the findings of previous studies together we proposed that social presence and interaction in the online classroom help to create what we began calling a "culture of community" (Perry & Edwards, 2009).

In sum, the findings of this initial program of research on the topic of exemplary educators revealed that exceptional online teachers foster interaction particularly among learners and between themselves and students, create a sense of social presence where they present themselves as 'real people' to the students, and establish a sense of community in the online courses they teach (Perry & Edwards, 2005).

The Aha Moment: It's About Humanity!

Next came an aha moment when Margaret and I realized a link between all the different teaching strategies outstanding educators used. One day we said to one another, "these educators are highly successful because they put their humanity into the online courses they teach." We noted that many of the approaches that the exemplary online teachers we studied used were arts-based and many included literary, visual, musical, or drama elements. The exemplary educators infused their courses with stories, poetry, craft-like activities, theme songs, re-enactments, role-playing, and photography. All of these elements were permeated with emotion and the human spirit and using these techniques to challenge the students brought a sense of genuine humanness to the learning milieu.

On further reflection, I noted that the approaches used by the exemplary online nurse educators who where our research participants paralleled my own attempts to make my online teaching more engaging – I recognized that I had also created teaching strategies that attempted to bring humanness to the virtual classrooms while also creating opportunities for learners to share their humanity with me and with one another other. For example, the instructional activity called photovoice (which I often used to stimulate discussion about a complex course topic in the class) used images which featured people and which were rich with the emotion of interpersonal communication. I used poetry (Haiku, rhyming verse, or free form) in my teaching which were ways "to communicate human emotion within the limitation of words" (van Manen, 1990, p. 22). Some of my preferred activities were the use of stories in various forms (oral, narrative, or words with images and music) to convey common human experiences that students could relate to because they had undergone similar circumstances in their lives.

So, it seemed the exemplary nurse educators who were excellent online teachers who were using instructional strategies instead, had a commonality of the foundation in the arts. I had also experienced a positive response from my students when I used arts-based approaches to teaching. When we put this together Margaret and I came up with a category of instructional strategies we called "artistic pedagogical technologies" (APTs) (Perry, Janzen, & Edwards, 2012). We set out to embark on a nationally funded multi-year study to explore the effects of APTs in online faculty of health disciplines courses (graduate level).

That's a Strange Acronym: What is an APT?

APTs are distinguished from traditional pedagogies by their emphasis on aesthetics and their heightened link to creativity (Perry & Edwards, 2009). Our subsequent research revealed the power and effect of APTs in online courses. For example, we found that APTs helped provide a real and authentic medium for instructors and students to engage with one other, with technology, and with the educational content. Further, a common theme in our research was that APTs helped to create inviting learning environments, in part because they initiated, sustained, and enhanced interaction between students and instructors and helped develop community (Janzen, Perry, & Edwards, 2012a). Further, the use of APTs stimulated creative thinking, captured student attention, extended the application of course content, contributed to positive learning outcomes, and helped develop a sense of professional fulfillment for instructors (Perry & Edwards, 2010). More positive consequences of APTs uncovered through research included that they contributed to students establishing a sense of group identity, supported course engagement, enhanced the learning environment, and developed social connectedness (Perry, Dalton, & Edwards, 2009). Finally, students reported a positive influence on not only course interactions, but on their sense of community, increased their comfort in the educational milieu, and research participants noted that APTs aided them in getting to know themselves, their classmates, and their instructors (Perry, Janzen, & Edwards, 2012b).

An Emerging Question: Why do APTs Work?

Now that we had an idea of *what* was occurring, we investigated *why* APTs have positive influences and found they helped create an "invitational" educational environment furthering learner engagement (Perry et al., 2012a). This brought us the "invitational education theory" (Purkey & Novak, 2015). Our conclusion was that APTs work in part because the learner engagement and sense of community helps create "invitational learning environments" (Perry et al., 2012a).

Soon, with the addition of Katherine Janzen to the team (who was initially the research assistant on our project and has since become the principal investigator on a follow-up study), the SITE mode was developed to further articulate why APTs are effective and eventually Katherine authored an emerging theory called QL (Janzen, Perry, & Edwards, 2016). We found an alignment between arts-based strategies and QL (Janzen et al., 2016).

The SITE Model. The SITE Model provided an additional theoretical framework and scaffolding for analysis and discussion of our ongoing research on APTs. The model illustrates how students, teachers, technology, and learning environments form an alliance which positively impacts learner engagement (Janzen et al., 2016). The SITE Model exemplifies this alliance in that it recognizes the necessity of the connection, communication, and interactivity between and among the SITE model's individual elements (students, instructor, technology, and environment) in order for quantum learning environments to exist. The SITE Model encapsulates the holistic/holographic integration of students, instructors, technology, and the quantum learning environment where attributes of Web 3.0 technology exist (Janzen et al., 2016). The attributes of Web 3.0 technology include empowerment, dynamic and interactive participation, flexibility, multi-dimensionality, multi-source content, personalization, user engagement, social involvement, and creativity (2016). ATPs are examples of teaching strategies that help create quantum learning environments by capitalizing on Web 3.0 attributes to further engage students (2016).

The Quantum Perspective of Learning (QL). Katherine's QL has moved our understanding of why APTs are effective forward. Online teaching and learning requires different new educational theory such as QL which moves beyond connectivism (where learning is the process of making connections) (Siemens, 2005) and constructivism (where learning is a product of social interaction) (Vygotsky, 1978) and suggests that everything is already connected and the processes of learning are bound up in discovering those connections (Janzen et al., 2016). In the past, the constructivist paradigm has played an important role in educational research. Discovering connections is posited to occur best in 'quantum learning environments' where students, instructors, technology, and learning environments become holistically integrated. Further, interaction within the quantum learning environment becomes a hallmark of QL where students are provided with opportunities and means to discover those connections (Janzen et al., 2016). There is more about QL and the link to APTs in later chapters.

Are APTs Effective in a Variety of Learning Environments and With Different Learner Levels?

Having the SITE Model and QL in place we felt we had substantiated that APTs have positive outcomes for teachers and learners in online learning environments, we understood some of the specific outcomes in more detail, we had a glimpse into why APTs have these positive outcomes, and we knew how various elements interacted to produce the benefits of APTs. As a team, we agreed that we had a strong foundation to continue to further our investigations related to APTs and to develop more tangible products of our research to share with other educators who might find this useful. This led to our ongoing national funded research project with Katherine as the principal investigator entitled, An exploration of the effects of arts-based teaching strategies on the engagement of digital native learners in online, blended, and face-to-face learning environments. All of our previous research had focused on online graduate-level learners, this study investigates the use of APTs in other learning milieu including face-to-face and hybrid classrooms. It also focuses on a different group of students – undergraduate level learners.

What's Next?

One practical outcome of our work that remains in process includes the development of an open-source repository of APTs that will be creative commons licensed for use or adaptation by educators worldwide. Others will have access to these free resources that can be easily adapted to multidisciplinary course content at the graduate or undergraduate level. Additionally, we plan to develop and share a set of research-informed recommendations for course design that incorporates APTs. Further, we plan to create additional APTs perhaps exploring how other arts and craft forms could be used as the foundation for specific learning strategies. To this point, we have created strategies primarily from the areas of music, photography, poetry, and story writing. We believe that other fields such as sculpture (physical or virtual), dance, architecture, and others could also provide impetus for new APTs. Another current study involves our use of weblogs and other social media based APTs in online teaching. With constant developments in virtual world technology, the possibilities for innovative APTs seem vast.

Based on our studies and experiences to this point, we believe that APTs could be used successfully (and yield strong positive benefits) in many types of learning environments, in a variety of fields of study, and with learners from kindergarten to post-graduate levels. Additional research will hopefully help us to substantiate this claim.

Conclusion

For now, we can say with evidence-informed confidence that APTs do aid learning and learner success in online graduate courses. We believe this is an important finding as the popularity of online education is expanding exponentially as the world becomes more technologically based. The Internet has changed the social and pedagogical perspective of learning (Shea, 2006). The new generation of learners has unique needs and perspectives and requires relevant and current course design and teaching strategies informed by educational theory suited to these learners and learning environments. Foundational shifts towards socio-cognitive theory and collaborative pedagogy are occurring and online courses and teaching should be in-line with these changes. Strategies such as APTs that enhance interaction, create a social presence, and build community through adding humanity to the course design and teaching are essential for educational success.

References

Janzen, K., Perry, B., & Edwards, M. (2012). The entangled web: Quantum learning, quantum learning environments and web technology. *Journal of Invitational Theory and Practice*, 4. Retrieved from ijq.cgpublisher.com

Janzen, K. J. (2013). Quantum learning environments: Making the virtual seem real in the online classroom. S. In *Melrose, C. Park, C., & B. Perry (Eds.) Teaching health professionals online: Frameworks and strategies*, 129-154.

Janzen, K.J., Perry, B., & Edwards, M. (2016). Building blocks: Enmeshing technology and creativity with artistic pedagogical technologies. *Turkish Online Journal of Education*. *18*(1). Retrieved from http://tojde.anadolu.edu.tr/next-issues-accepted-articles-.html

Kant, K. (2012). The future of higher education: M-learning. *Indian Streams Research Journal*, *2*(11), 1-7.

Perry, B., & Edwards, M. (2005). Exemplary online educators: Creating a community of inquiry. *Turkish Online Journal of Distance Education*, 6(2). Retrieved from http://tojde.anadolu.edu.tr/tojde18/articles/article6.htm

Perry, B., & Edwards, M. (2009). Strategies for creating virtual learning communities. In *Nursing and Clinical Informatics: Socio-Technical Approaches*, B. Staudinger, V. Hob, H. Ostrmeann, (Eds.). (pp.175-197). Hersey, CA: IGI Global. www.igi-global.com

Perry, B., Dalton, J., & Edwards, M. (2009). Photographic images as an interactive online teaching technology: Creating online communities. *International Journal of Teaching and Learning in Higher Education*, *20(2)*, 106-115.

Perry, B., & Edwards, M. (2010). Creating a culture of community in the online classroom using artistic pedagogical technologies. *Using Emerging Technologies in Distance Education*. G. Veletsianos (Ed.). Edmonton, AB: AU Press. (book chapter). Retrieved from http://www.veletsianos.com/2010/11/14/data-on-our-open-access-book/

Perry, B., Janzen, K., & Edwards, M. (2012a). Creating invitational online learning environments using learning interventions founded in the arts. *Opening Learning Horizons*. http://elearningpapers.eu/en/elearning_papers

Perry, B., & Edwards, M., & Janzen, K. (2012b). Using invitational theory to understand the effectiveness of artistic pedagogical technologies in online distance education classrooms. Proceedings of the Hawaii International Conference on Education. Honolulu, HI, January 5-8.

Purkey, W., & Novak, J. (2015). An introduction to invitational theory. Retrieved from https://www.invitationaleducation.net/docs/samples/art_intro_to_invitational_theory.pdf

Rourke, L., Anderson T., Garrison, D.R., & Archer, W. (2001). Assessing social presence in asynchronous text-based computer conferencing. *Journal of Distance Education, 14*(3), 51-70.

Siemens, G. (2005). Connectivism: A learning theory for the digital age. *International Journal of Instructional Technology & Distance Learning, 2*(1). Retrieved from http://www.itdl.org/Journal/Jan_05/article01.htm

Shea, P. (2006). In online environments. *Journal of Asynchronous Learning Network, 10*(1). Retrieved from http://www.sloan-c.org/publications/jaln/v10n1/v10n1_4shea.asp

UNESCO (2012). Turning on mobile learning in North America. Retrieved from http://unesdoc.unesco.org/images/0021/002160/216083E.pdf

Van Manen, M. (1990). *Researching human experience*. London, ON: Althouse Press.

Vygotsky, L. S. (1978). *Mind in society: The development of higher psychological processes*. (M. Cole, V. John-Steiner, S. Scribner, & E. Souberman, Eds.). Cambridge, Massachusetts: Harvard University Press.

Chapter 2

Theoretical Foundations: The Quantum Perspective of Learning

Katherine J. Janzen

Background

Now with over 13 years of research behind us on APTs (see Chapter 5), our research has lent much support to the conclusion that APTs 'work' in classrooms. In 2010, we asked the question, "Why do APTs work?" The answer was not easily forthcoming. At the time I was finishing my Master's degree in nursing and working as a research assistant for Beth and Margaret. I took this question to heart. It troubled me so greatly that I lost sleep thinking about it. The question seemed to consume my thoughts. We knew that APTs had many positive benefits for learners but what was the reason that they had this helpful influence on students and the educational environment?

One October night in 2010 I was working in the role of night Charge Nurse on an acute care orthopedic trauma unit. It was not a busy night which was unusual for that unit. During the quietest time of the night, I had time to ponder once again the question or the underlying reason for the effectiveness of APTs. The orange moon was not the only thing that was burning brightly that night. As I sat and pondered, thoughts came rushing into my mind and I quickly scribbled them down on a piece of paper. Suddenly I had an answer - I knew why APTs worked!

That night, the five assumptions of the Quantum Perspective of Learning (QL) were born. I emailed Beth the next day and told her I knew why APTs worked in the classroom. I also told her I would start to write a paper on this topic and email it to her as soon as I could. I found sleep difficult in the next few weeks. Even the need for food became secondary at times as I wrote. Hours would go by and I would lose all sense of time. My thoughts even invaded my dreams.

I would find myself dreaming about a concept and waking in the middle of the night (often several times a night) to reflect on an emerging idea. I would write the ideas in a little black book I kept on my night table beside my bed. I truly felt inspired to write. I also felt inspired to read and study all I could about quantum physics and its related theories.

Upon finishing the paper, I sent it to Beth to read. After a few days of waiting for a reply from Beth, her email came. She told me she had sent the paper to Margaret, and Beth confided to me that it was the most excited that she had seen Margaret in some time. Margaret and Beth were indeed excited about the emerging theory and encouraged me to enlarge this inaugural paper into five papers on the topic.

Margaret also suggested that we hold a salon, much like the salons of the 17th and 18th centuries which were held in Europe—where great thinkers gathered in the home of an inspiring host and shared discussions related to literature, philosophy or other aspects of their work and thinking.

Margaret arranged for a salon to be held in Calgary at her home with great thinkers from several departments at Athabasca University present. I presented my theory of the QL to them.

The response at first was silence, as if everyone was deep in thought and trying to make sense by applying the theory to their own experiences in teaching and learning. Eventually, questions were asked, and a brisk and enlightening discussion ensued. Those present unanimously agreed that QL fit with their experiences with online education.

As I discussed QL with each in attendance at the salon, each professor encouraged me to develop QL and write a series of papers on the subject. I proceeded to do so. Over the next few months I wrote feverishly. Every spare minute I had was spent pondering, writing, and then pondering again. I consulted Beth often with my thinking as she acted as my mentor, edited my papers, and asked me more questions to think upon. Both Beth and Margaret were instrumental in the publication of these papers. These were exciting times for me. I often felt myself catching my breath in anticipation.

In the ensuing three years, four of the five papers were published in respectable, peer-reviewed journals (Janzen, Perry & Edwards, 2011a; 2012a; 2012b; 2012c). A fifth paper was added exploring 'how' APTs work (Janzen, Perry & Edwards, 2017). A sixth paper is now written and submitted for publication.

In 2013, I was invited to write a chapter on the QL in the book, *Teaching Health Professionals Online: Frameworks and Strategies*, (Melrose, Park, & Perry, 2013). Several more papers have been written and published using

Theoretical Foundations 11

the QL as a theoretical framework (Edwards. Perry, Janzen & Menzies, 2012; Janzen, Szabo & Jakubec, 2016; Janzen et al., 2017). The papers are now being cited in other authors' work.

Today the work continues in a nationally funded, five-year study exploring the use of APTs in online, face-to-face and blended classrooms. I continue to be amazed when I reflect on how QL has evolved over the past 8 years. That idea that came to me in the wee hours of the morning one dark October night has come to serve as a foundation of our research and for the investigations led by other academics. In this chapter QL is explored as the theoretical foundation of APTs. First, however, a basic understanding of quantum mechanics may be of great value for you.

Quantum Mechanics: A Reference Point

The word quantum is ubiquitous in our world today. A simple search using the keyword "quantum" on Google Scholar ™ reveals myriads of papers, written from various viewpoints, on almost infinite topics. Writers in disciplines from ecology to leadership focus on quantum something. It is a popular and often used term, but what does quantum, and in particular quantum mechanics, actually mean?

To an educator, the axioms of quantum mechanics may seem to be derived from an episode of Star Trek™, rather than being fundamental to an educational theory. These axioms include diatomic lithium molecules, matter-wave devaluation, neutron crystal beam splitters and nano particle interference (Arndt & Hornberger, 2014). The relationship of these maxims to education will become clearer as I explain each in term in the following paragraphs. First, it is important to define quantum physics as the foundation for examining the five following axioms: waves, particles and superposition, entanglement and the future of quantum physics.

Griffiths (2016) quotes two physicists: Richard Feynman who said, "I think I can safely say that no one understands quantum mechanics," and Niels Bohr who commented that, "If you are not confused by quantum physics, then you really haven't understood it" (p. vii). This really does encompass quantum mechanics in a nutshell! The more I read and study quantum mechanics, the more I realize that there is so much more out there to know and I have barely touched the surface of the knowledge we as human beings have concerning it. I humbly admit that although many times I am left more confused than with understanding, quantum mechanics has a certain appeal to me; I am always left thinking and considering the possibilities regarding how it applies to teaching and learning.

Waves and Particles, Superposition and Entanglement

> *Reality cannot be found except in One single source, because of the interconnection of all things with one another.* (Leibniz, 1670/2012)

For the non-physicist, quantum mechanics can be reduced to a single maxim: everything is connected. Quantum mechanics extends from the scale of the micro world of atoms, electrons, neutrons and protons (Pinto-Neto & Struyev, 2018), to the mesocosm of our earth, to the vast confines of the macrocosm of the universe. Quantum mechanics demonstrates a sense of connectedness for the biggest of big and the smallest of small (Onishi, 2018; Navascués, Guryanova, Hoban & Acín, 2014). This connectedness results in a state of constant communication between the micro, the meso and the macro (Aczel, 2001).

All that we know exists microscopically, temporally or universally. All things (even that which we have no knowledge of), are proposed to be an "intricate system of communication and information exchange" (Janzen et al., 2012a, p. 2; Pribram, 2006). Three terms encapsulate quantum mechanics: entanglement, superposition, and waves and particles.

De Broglie (1962) in his seminal work on waves and particles used the example of a musical instrument to understand waves and particles in a simplified manner. I will begin with an explanation of waves and particles using an example of a violin (Janzen, 2012a). Think for a moment about a violin. The violin, when a bow is set upon the strings, produces tones and overtones. The tones and overtones could be considered to be waves which emit from the violin's strings. While tones and overtones are produced the violin remains as a single instrument. Thus, the violin is holistic in nature. In other words, "The violin, while it is the propagator of the wave (tones/overtones) cannot be separated from the violin" (p, 2).

The ocean provides another example of this interconnection. The ocean is made up of water (particles) which produces waves as the water reaches the shore. One does not think of the ocean as separable from either the water or the waves. They are one, they embody holism. These waves and particles communicate with each other and are in constant connection. This communication exists in all things great and small—whether this be atoms or the universe.

All that exists in the universe could be considered to be a giant spider web which has no beginning or end, or in other words, it is boundaryless (Janzen, 2012a). The strands of the spider web connect all that exists. The interesting thing is that in quantum holism there are no empty spaces between the strands (as there is in a spider's web). The seemingly empty spaces are filled with energy which communicates and is connected. Thus, holism exists in all things.

Superposition suggests that when waves "travel through a medium, they combine to produce a product wave in which the original waves produce an interference pattern" (Hwang, 2011; Janzen et al., 2012a, p. 2). Hwang proposes that maintenance of integrity in the waves of origin, as well as the subsequent combination of other waves results in unique patterns which differ from the original waves. This unique pattern (or patterns) of waves allows for an electron, atom or neutron to exist at more than two places at once (Arntz, Chasse & Vincente, 2006). I use the example of an individual being in a room with two doors (Janzen et al., 2012b).

Superposition allows an individual to be able to exit the room through both doors at the same time. Amazing? Not with atoms, electrons or neutrons! (Aczel, 2002). Slit barrier experiments have shown that when a single electron, neutron or atom goes through a barrier with two slits in it, the electron, neutron or atom goes through both slits at the same time (Arntz et al., 2006).

The last term that defines quantum mechanics, and provides the necessary building blocks to better understand quantum holism, is that of entanglement. Plank found that the spaces between particles (think of the spider's web) were made up of energy (Arntz et al., 2006; Janzen et al., 2012b). Harokpos (2005) further proposed that "all phenomenon are caused by energy transfer" (p. 90). This energy transfer is explained by entanglement. Entanglement is a very basic form means that everything that exists is connected (Janzen et al., 2012a).

For example, to make gravy from a roast, one must take the juices from the roast and combine them with flour, salt, pepper and water to form a whole. It is through the stirring of the gravy, and the addition of heat (both being forms of energy transfer) that causes the parts (juices, flour, salt, pepper and water) to become one to change and transform the very liquid juices of the roast into a semi-thickened gravy. When the final product is ready, all elements are connected, and in essence, communicate with each other. No longer are we left with parts, but we have wholes. This example illustrates entanglement, waves and particles, and superposition and ties all three terms into quantum holism. Entanglement is illustrated in that everything in the gravy is connected. Waves and particles are demonstrated in that the gravy is made up of particles which in their presentation create gravy which is pourable (waves). Superposition is illustrated in that the salt, pepper and flour are all in superposition with one another.

The Future of Quantum Physics

As a theory, "the validity of quantum mechanics in the microscopic and mesoscopic realm has been established up to incredible precision" (Navascués et al., 2014, p. 1). Within the macroscopic realm, "where the universe is described by quantum theory . . . we are sentient physical systems living in such a universe" (Sudbery, 2017, p. 4451). We are, in essence, "living in [a] quantum world" (p. 4430) that exists within a not so quiet quantum information revolution (Arndt & Hornberger, 2014; Khrennikov, De Raedt, Plotnisky & Polyakov, 2015).

Quantum physics has intrigued scientists and philosophers alike, because it

> challenges our notions of reality and locality—concepts we have come to rely on in our macroscopic world. Scientific progress over the last decades inspires. . . hope. (Arndt & Hornberger, 2014, p. 271)

To this end, the last 30 years have brought much knowledge and progress in the field of quantum mechanics (Arndt & Hornberger, 2014). To illustrate this, China in 2016, launched a quantum communications satellite, the first of its kind in the world (Zaminspira & Niknamian, 2017). This satellite is capable of testing quantum communication between earth and space and has the potential to test entanglement over what is considered to be "unprecedented distances" (p. 15). Early results in June of 2017 reveal the distance of entanglement is 1203 kilometers (Yin et al., 2017). The future, it seems, is wrapped up in quantum mechanics. The potential to understand learning using a foundation of quantum physics principles is intriguing.

The Quantum Perspective of Learning: Assumptions and Principles

Although quantum mechanics may be best understood by students of physics and mathematics, physicist David Bohm (1917-1992) explained quantum mechanics in a way that it made perfect sense to me in terms of learning. His eloquent papers drew me in immediately as he wrote of elemental faucets of quantum mechanics and holism that could be readily understood by someone who has only completed physics and mathematics at a high school level. Bohm's writings spoke of the familiar and the everyday. It was from Bohm's (1971; 1973) papers that QL was extended from a primordial set of assumptions to a perspective of learning.

The Quantum Perspective of Learning (QL) has five assumptions which guide application to APTs:

1. Learning is multidimensional.
2. Learning occurs in several planes simultaneously.
3. Learning consists of potentialities which exist infinitely
4. Learning is both holistic and holographic and is patterned within holographic realities.
5. Learning environments are living systems. (Janzen et al., 2011a, p. 64)

Seven principles are identified which further expand upon the five assumptions. These principles originally pertained to online learning and online learning environments only. However, through further research, we now believe that these assumptions have equal applicability to face-to-face and blended learning and learning environments. The seven principles are:

1. The essence of learning is multidimensional construction. As we accept that we are holistic beings, then our teaching and learning will center on a multitude of dimensions.
2. Holistic development occurs in and through learning. This learning must occur within innumerable planes of dimensions to encourage holistic development. If we as educators reach students solely in one quantum dimension (e.g., cognitive or emotive) is not adequate to stimulate learning. Rather it is necessary to encourage learning that outspreads beyond the boundaries of classrooms. If multiple dimensions are reached learning becomes lifelong. In short, learning becomes something that is not forgotten once students leave the classroom.
3. There is an infinite potential to learn and to develop in all quantum dimensions. This is true of all human beings.
4. The potential of all human beings to learn is everywhere. Being separated geographically or asynchronously can be seen to be a potentiality instead of a limitation.
5. Holographic realities should align themselves with instructional design in order to further learners' grasps into holographic realities. Their realities extend far beyond temporality and virtuality. Holistic realities and thus holistic education, then, become an interface between students, teachers, technology, and the environment.
6. Through time and space, the learning environments which are living, growing, evolving and developing entities, become

dynamic environments which support not only the needs of educational system, but also the needs of teachers and learners.
7. Transformation of educators, students and educational environments can transpire through the passage of time. Technology likewise can be transformed in a direct and indirect manner through the alterations that occur through students, teachers and educative environments. (Janzen et al., 2011a).

The Quantum Perspective of Learning: An Orientation

Within QL educators are called upon to transcend the world as we visually know it through our natural senses. Educators move into the realms of quantum physics: the world of the electron and atoms; quarks and quanta. QL borrows select concepts from quantum physics and applies them to learning and learning environments. As a caveat, QL is not a theory of quantum physics, but rather I have found key elements which mimic learning as I have searched the literature (new and old) related to quantum physics. What has resulted, is a perspective that can open educators' minds and cause them to view learning in new ways. As educators apply QL using APTs, their teaching can enliven classrooms, and engage students. In the end, is not student engagement one of the primary goals of teaching and learning?

To understand QL more fully, we present three areas for you to consider: (1) realms of knowledge and definitions related to QL (Janzen et al., 2012b), (2) quantum learning environments and the SITE Model (Janzen et al., 2012a), and (3) "cues and conduits to learning" through quantum dimensions (Janzen et al., 2012c, p. 119; Janzen, Perry & Edwards, 2017).

Concept One: QL Definitions and The Realms of Knowledge

Definitions

It would be impossible to enter into a discussion of QL without first understanding the definitions which guide the basic constructs or building blocks of QL: quanta, quantum, quantum dimensions and quantum states. Quanta manifests itself as the smallest unit of learning. Quantum represents several units grouped together. Quantum can be large or small in nature— ranging from tiny, imperceptible bits to the infinite expanse.

Quantum dimensions are those that we conceptualize as knowledge which arises from learning. These dimensions include: behavioral, cognitive, social, spiritual, technological, emotional, experiential, corporeality, and cultural learning/knowledge. It is known that we each learn in different ways. Each quantum dimension represents a way, or a conduit, to learning.

We posit that the more quantum dimensions that can be touched upon by an instructor in a nursing classroom, the greater the potential for students in that classroom to learn.

Quantum states are those states upon which learning is predicated or occurs. Educators can make their classrooms places or spaces that are conducive to learning. Quantum states are those in which the environment plays a great part. We believe that quantum states are created by educators when they make their classrooms inviting to students. Within an optimal quantum state, students' learning is maximized; within a sub-optimal quantum state, learning can be less than desired.

The Realms of Knowledge

> *We imagine posthumans as humans made superhumanly intelligent or resilient by future advances in nanotechnology, biotechnology, information technology and cognitive science. Many argue that these enhanced people might live better lives; others fear that tinkering with our nature will undermine our sense of our own humanity.*
>
> -David Roden, 2015

To begin to understand learning, we begin by describing an understanding of the realms of knowledge. It has been known for decades that "human beings only use a fraction of their mental" capacities (Janzen et al., 2012b, p. 5; Roden, 2015). This is supported by Arntz (2006) who states that the human awareness processes 2,000 bits of information per second, while there are four billion bits of information that the mind processes per second. While Roden posits that in the future science, medicine, and technology may be destined to be mediated to create posthumans or Humans 2.0, at this time in the millennium we know that we have only scratched the surface of human potential. There are myriads of resources, both information/technology and educators/mentors, to help us to learn, develop, and grow. To think of this simply, the third assumption of QL (learning consists of infinite potentialities), captures this idea.

Learning can be conceptualized as knowledge. Within QL, knowledge is made up of four components. These are distinct and separate and yet each component communicates with all the other components and ultimately the collection is circumscribed as intelligence. These realms of knowledge include quantasic, atomistic, temporalistic, and universalistic knowledge. The realms of knowledge can be represented as four, holographic octagons nested within each other. Each octagon communicates with the others and shares information.

The first component, the quantasic realm of knowledge, happens where intelligence first resides. Intelligence is found within the smallest units of learning—quanta—and is the innermost part of the octagon. Everything (large and small) are made up of quanta, and when grouped into units of quanta, they become apparent as quantum. These quanta are the basic building blocks of learning.

The second component, the atomistic realm of knowledge, is knowledge that manifests itself in structures that cannot be seen with the naked eye. The atomistic realm of knowledge is represented in the second octagon. This knowledge is sought and realized using technology and is microscopic in nature. Intelligence here is seen in neural pathways and synapses, and in the re-wiring of those pathways as we learn and develop (Pert, 1997). Pert describes an emotional response in terms of molecules. Emotional responses can, and often do, accompany deep learning which in turn reinforces that learning or strengthens that neural learning pathway. The continuous creation of new neural pathways results in an infinite ability for perpetual learning.

This continuous learning begins before a baby is born. We learn in utero from both parental and environmental stimuli (Stratford, Compton & Wagg, 2017). This is well demonstrated in research and is not limited to learning related to: linguistics (Avishai-Eliner, Sandman & Baram, 2002), stress (Bates, Thal, Lindley & Clancy, 1995), voice and language recognition, food and flavor preferences, thinking, relating, emotions, and music recognition (Stratford, Compton & Wagg, 2017). For example, my daughter played calming music while she was expecting her first child, especially when the fetus was overactive. This soothed the fetus greatly. Even after birth, the baby boy was always calmed by this same music. We learn as well until the end of life, and perhaps in life after life, in this instance in temporality.

The temporalistic realm of knowledge is found within the third octagon. The temporalistic realm of knowledge is the knowledge that pertains to this earth—all that we know, and all that we can come to know through scientific discoveries and our own personal learning pursuits. Intelligence is found within the temporalistic realm as well. It is posited that every individual (or everything that exists) has intelligence. In humans, intelligence is not measured by the intelligence quotient (IQ) but rather by

Theoretical Foundations

the ongoing capacity to learn, grow and develop. Our intelligence can be expanded by through all of our senses.

Last, the universalistic realm of knowledge is that knowledge that pertains to the cosmos. It is found within the fourth and last octagon. One just has to look at images taken through high powered telescopes, and images that have been sent back to us from space exploration (human in the form of space travel/space stations, and non-human in the form of satellites which orbit other planets), to know that universalistic intelligence exists. Through the wonder of these images and space communication we continue to understand the magnitude of universalistic knowledge.

Each of these realms of knowledge consists of parts and wholes at the same time, just as Bohm (1971; 1973) described. As we look at the great expanse of the universe, we are aware there is something greater than ourselves. This occurs within all realms of knowledge. Discoveries in the future will add more perspective to each realm of knowledge. To us, it is astonishing to think that even 10 years from now we will know more within the realms of all types of knowledge. To illustrate this, consider that technology is often outdated before it comes to the market. The future is very bright as each realm of knowledge communicates with the other realms and we continually discover and understand more about ourselves, others and the micro, the meso, and the macro. Our potential to become, not just be is only now in our imaginations.

Concept Two: Quantum Learning Environments and the SITE Model

We live in a world of complexity where few things are simple. In our everyday lives, we use all our senses as we learn about that complexity through television, technology or other forms of social media. At times it can seem overwhelming with so much information coming at us. Where we as educators we were once relinquished to the use of encyclopaedias and text books for our students, the Internet has opened so many avenues of learning--literally using our fingertips. What once used to fill volumes of written materials or music now has been reduced to a four by six-inch cell phone which can hold textbooks, emails and thousands of songs. Data is no longer expressed in terms of research, but now in terms of gigabytes of data which is sometimes utilized daily by our students.

For seasoned educators, it might seem that potential ways and means of teaching students are limitless and overwhelming through the rapid expanse of technology which changes each year. For those educators who are technologically savvy, technology could be considered the way of not only the future but the way of the now. Technology, however, does not alone make for great teaching or learning. There are other factors at play. This portion of this chapter focuses on the creation of quantum learning environments and the SITE Model (Janzen et al., 2012a) as a way of understanding those environments more fully.

Quantum Learning Environments. Quantum Learning Environments or QLEs satisfy the QL requirements of being an environment and a system simultaneously. An environment is any form of matter or milieu in which learning occurs. These include micro, meso, and macro environments. You also may have discovered that living systems are those that are "open, self-organizing [and have] special characteristics of life and [interaction] with their environment . . . by means of information exchanges" (Parent, 2000, para 2).

We often associate learning with the animate, but research has established that learning can occur with the inanimate (Deng, 2018; Hodges, 2018). This can be demonstrated by a computer. A computer, as a form of artificial intelligence (AI), can learn user preferences or even learn to program itself and act upon that programming (Cohen & Feigenbaum, 2014). To this end, a computer learns. According to the definition given above, a computer is a living system. Cohen and Feigenbaum state, "A computer must be able to sense its environment, have a memory and must learn, it should construct rudimentary plans to solve problems, and it should be able to reason inductively and deductively" (p. xiv). Does this sound futuristic? Yet, AI is already all around us—especially in health care (Hodges, 2018). Eventually, AI is expected to replace some of the jobs that are routinely done in health care (Hodges, 2018; King 2018). Scary? Perhaps, but think of what the future may hold for technological developments to help educators!

QLEs, in the context of this chapter, are focused on creating living environments that evolve, breathe (metaphorically), and grow. QLEs are not stagnant. I use the metaphor of a pond to illustrate this (Janzen et al., 2012a). On a hot summer's day when there is no breeze, a pond at a short distance could seem to be a stagnant environment. A simple look into the pond begs difference as the pond is actually a living milieu for all types of organisms which interact with not only the pond, but with each other, elements in a complex ecosystem of the pond, the air above and the land which forms a boundary around the pond. The boundaries of the pond are not static—the pond enlarges when it rains and shrinks in periods of drought. If thought of in terms of QL, if everything is connected from the small to the large, then the boundaries are only quasi-rigid in nature (Bohm, 1971) and extend infinitely.

In QLEs the boundaries are not static either. Classroom environments can enlarge or shrink depending upon the care taken to maintain the life of the QLE or to create conditions that lead to QLE growth. It takes the effort of all that is contained within the QLE to do this in a sense of cooperation, imagination and creativity (see Chapter 3). The primary constitutes of a QLE are students, instructors, technology and environment and are expressed in terms of the Student-Instructor-Technology-Environment (SITE) Model.

The SITE Model. In classrooms, QLEs are developed and influenced by the students themselves. Much of this development takes place within the confines of the classroom but can extend outside the classroom as well as students are exposed to precepts of QL. Student engagement could be seen as paramount in the intersection of all other elements of the SITE Model. Learning can become fun as students engage with the environment, other students, the instructor, and the environment. The outputs of creativity and imagination are at their maximum in QLEs as students learn to play and play to learn within that environment (see Chapter 3 for more about play and creativity). Learning begins to become fun again for students. Previous knowledge and attitudes toward learning affect QLEs as all that the student brings to the nursing classroom can either attract or detract from the environment.

Factors related to the instructor include all the attributes of Garrison, Anderson and Archer's Community of Inquiry Model (CoI) (Garrison, 2016). These attributes are: social presence, cognitive presence, teaching presence, and their subsets of supporting outcomes, selecting content, and setting climate. In CoIs all of the above attributes and their subsets intersect into educator experience. Pollard, Minor and Swanson (2014) suggest a fourth attribute: teacher social presence which has implications for QLEs, especially in online learning environments where instructor-student and student-peer social presence improved the learning experience and made it 'real.' Within our own research, we concur with Pollard and colleagues' conclusions (Janzen, Perry & Edwards, 2011b). For the SITE Model the ease of use of technology and the level of technology utilized by the instructor are vital and border on the other three components of the model.

As technology has become a mainstay of our society today, students come well versed in various forms of technology as it is always at their fingertips. This creates students who can be versatile in whatever medium that is chosen to assist learning. At times students have a much greater capacity for technology utilization than their instructors do! Technology, however, need not be a deterrent for teaching or learning. Technology can come in the simplest of forms such as felt pens and paper or more complex forms such as computer programs and programming. APTs used in QLEs focus primarily on the simple, the familiar, and manipulate those forms of low technology to their maximum potential.

The actual physical environment of the classroom or the larger university environment influence learning as well. Fraser (2015) claims that "extensive past research provides consistent evidence that the classroom environment is so consistently associated with student outcomes that it should not be ignored by those wishing to improve the [student and teacher experience]" (p 154). The environment extends past the classroom into the clinical setting where QLEs can also exist. Papathanasiou, Tsaras and Sarafis (2014) explored nursing students' perceptions and views regarding clinical learning environments. They found that there was a significant difference between student expectations and realities and recommended that more emphasis be placed upon innovation and individualization (p. 57). These conclusions could readily be extended into face-to-face, blended and online classrooms. It is posited that QLEs through the use of APTs, provide both individualization and innovation in education.

Ultimately, the intersection of students, instructor, technology, and environment forms a QLE. In the QLE, students and instructors can be free to grow and learn from one another. Learning in a QLE can become a space of wonder and awe as students discover themselves, technology, the environment, and their instructors in new ways which potentiate the cues and conduits to learning.

Concept Three: Cues and Conduits to Learning

The cues and conduits to learning can be simply understood as quantum dimensions which are acted upon, or being acted upon, in relation to students (Janzen et al., 2017a). Quantum dimensions are the intersection of cognitive, behavioral, social, cultural, spiritual, technological, and other dimensions which together create a unified whole, which in this case is a human being or student. Essentially, the various quantum dimensions are ways of learning.

Students learn in a variety of ways. Thus, it becomes prudent to reach students with as many quantum dimensions in a given semester as possible to promote deep learning. In this kind of learning it is imperative to reach not only a certain subset of students, but all students within a classroom.

Each quantum dimension 'fills in the spaces' of student learning. If an educator can touch upon as many quantum dimensions as possible, learning may be enhanced for those learners who do not learn in traditional ways such as through lectures. This can culminate in a more positive learning experience for students and can heighten learner engagement (Janzen et al., 2012c). Largely, enacting the quantum dimensions, or putting them into action, involves 'doing' instead of simply 'listening.' Reaching into the quantum dimensions involves students in their learning where they can apply APTs to what is being taught. This may have implications for knowledge retention if APTs are linked to particular concepts. Types of APTs, and how to utilize them in a classroom, will be discussed in detail in Chapter four.

The Relationship between Artistic Pedagogical Technologies and the Quantum Perspective of Learning

Since that night in October 2010 when I was working the night shift at the hospital, I have continued to ponder upon the question that Beth and Margaret posed to me. Why do APTs work? In the final section of this chapter, we present 10 maxims that summarize why we believe APTs work.

1. APTs help sustain and contribute to the growth of QLEs.

The second law of thermodynamics centers on the concept of entropy. Entropy broadly suggests that there is ultimately a "degree of disorder or uncertainty in a system" (Merriam Webster, 2018, para. 1). If a system is not growing, it is decaying. Likewise, if a classroom is not growing, it is decaying, and learning can be impacted. QLEs are living systems where growth can and should occur.

2. The infusion of APTs to QLEs allows all quantum dimensions to be utilized within a given classroom (Janzen et al., 2011a).

It is well known that students learn in different ways. These ways are commonly expressed as kinesthetic, auditory, visual or psychomotor styles of learning. QL posits that students learn in, and through, quantum dimensions which have an impact on learning. Where one quantum dimension appeals to a certain subset of students, another dimension may appeal to another subset. The use of APTs, which target all quantum dimensions over a course or a semester, increases the likelihood that learning will occur for a maximum number of learners.

3. APTs provide the building blocks necessary to help connect existing concepts in a deeper way (Janzen et al., 2017).

While Siemens (2006) suggests that learning is the process of making connections, in QL the process of learning involves discovering the connections between all that exists. All connections already exist, it is just that students have not discovered these connections yet. APTs allow students 'aha' moments when everything comes together (as they discover existing connections) and suddenly something that was once confusing now makes sense.

4. APTs use ordinary and familiar objects to stimulate learning (Janzen, 2013).

The research on APTs support these activities that students participate in need not be grand in nature, expensive, or involve the latest technology (Janzen et al., 2017). Simple objects such as paper and felt pens, Lego™, or Playdough™ can stimulate the minds of students leading to expressions of creativity. Familiar objects, used in a purposeful way by skilled educators, can allow students to see concepts in new ways.

5. APTs start where students are at (Janzen, 2013).

As in the previous maxim, felt pens and paper have been used with students since primary school. While in primary school objects such as felt pens took time to master with ease, students in post-secondary education already come with these skills. APTs use previous experience with a medium, object or image as a taking off point to learning in new ways.

6. APTs help create a fundamental belief that that students and educators can succeed. (Janzen et al., 2017).

In my experience with using APTs (and teaching other educators how to use APTs) students and educators can be quite tentative at first. After experience with one APT, students begin to look forward to continued opportunities to employ APTs in their learning. For example, an educator reported that students were "very engaged" when she used a particular APT and she was "really excited" about the use of further APTs in her classroom (personal communication, J. Bouma, January 15, 2012). In APTs there is no right or wrong way to do an activity, and there is often no right or wrong answer or outcome. This non-judgemental aspect of APTs frees learners to engage in APTs without fear of failure, something uncommon in most traditional approaches to learning.

One semester teaching in a six-week intensive nursing course I wrote personal expressions of appreciation on thank you cards for each student in relation to an APT they had participated in over the term. The cards expressed my confidence in each student's ability to succeed in nursing and noted the special gifts and talents that I observed in each learner. Did it take time? Yes, but it was worth every minute spent writing those cards. That feedback energized them a time when they were struggling with the intensity of the course and the resultant heavy workload. I had several emails from students thanking me for the hope that the cards had given them. My words propelled them to complete the course, and ultimately to succeed.

7. APTs can increase the confidence of both students and instructors (Janzen et al., 2017).

When I first started to use APTs in face-to-face classrooms, APTs had only been studied and tested in online learning environments by Margaret and Beth. As an expert practitioner in the hospital setting, I had transitioned into being a nurse educator at a mid-sized university. It took courage for me to use APTs during the first semester as I began my new role as a classroom teacher. Each time I used an APT her confidence increased, and I was willing and excited to try more APTs as the semester progressed. Initially, students were hesitant to try APTs, but since 2011 I have not had any students refuse to engage in an APT. As each APT was presented throughout the semester, students gained confidence in their ability to express their feelings and ideas through APTs. Instead of saying, "What do we *have* to do today?" students began saying, "What do we *get* to do today?" The feedback provided to the students on the various APTs they engaged in was meaningful to them and the success was reflected back to me in student evaluations of instruction completed at the end of the term. My confidence in using these creative (and some would say unorthodox) instructional strategies grew along with my abilities to succeed as an educator.

8. APTs encourage creativity (Janzen et al., 2017).

In one APT exercise, we used Playdough™ with students to emphasize the concept of burnout. Students were asked to sculpt what burnout looked like. When students were done sculpting, they then took turns sharing their creations with the other students and speaking to their sculptures. The connections were very deep (and higher-order thinking evident) as students took lecture material and their understanding of it and integrated it into their explanations of their sculptures. I was left in awe with their creativity and how deeply they really connected with burnout in nursing.

9. APTs are innovative and engaging (Edwards et al., 2012).

As Papathanasiou and colleagues (2014) described, nursing students desire innovative ways of learning, especially in the clinical setting. Parsons and Taylor in 2011 reported that disengagement has been cited "to be one of the most pervasive challenges in education today" (Janzen et al., 2012c, p. 117). By using APTs in a classroom or clinical setting, students can appreciate the innovative nature of APTs. Through the research that has been done utilizing the creative arts, engagement has been reported to be a solid outcome time after time (Janzen, MacLean & Wiebe, 2016; Janzen et al., 2017; Perry, Edwards & Janzen, 2016; Perry, Janzen & Edwards, 2012).

10. APTs can result in 'meaning-making' and provides opportunities for reflection in students (Perry et al., 2016; Szabo, Jakubec & Janzen, 2017).

APTs allow the transfer of course material to a creative art-based medium and then back again as students reflect upon the activity they have just completed. I enjoy teaching nursing theoretical foundations and leadership courses. The content of these courses invites the use of APTs. APTs allow students to 'say' things through their APT and to express ideas or feelings that may be difficult to share using traditional teaching approaches. This expression of deep-seeded thoughts allows the quantum dimension of emotions to be shared safely. While some outputs of APTs are shared with their peers, most of the APTs are only shared with the instructor. This develops a milieu of trust between instructor and student and encourages a reflective cycle. For example, in using reflective journaling in the clinical setting, students are given the opportunity to reflect upon their day in clinical. Their reflections are often profound and filled with emotion. This APT gives an opportunity for meaning-making for students as they not only express their feelings but have personalized feedback from their instructor in return. The feedback includes specific questions to stimulate additional thought and further reflection as the cycle continues.

At the universities where we teach, the curriculum for first-year clinical allows for the use of APTs in any form that students choose. We have received some stunning (and touching) poetry from students that caused us to cry. The ability students have to express essential aspects of nursing care (and what they have learned about being a nurse) through APTs is profound. We honor the students' willingness to take risks, and their capacity to trust, as they share their APTs with us.

This chapter has come full circle now, from the beginning to the end and back again. We have explored the theoretical foundations of APTs and the landscapes of QL. We are struck with the excitement we feel when we think about QL. It truly is as Eliot (2011) said, we come once more to know the places and spaces of QL for the very first time. It is the possibilities that take our breath away.

> *And to make an end is to make a beginning. The end is where we start from... We shall not cease from exploration, and the end of all our exploring will be to arrive where we started and know the place for the first time.* (T.S. Eliot, 2011)

Now that a basic explanation of QL has been presented, one question may endure: What is the significance of QL? One simple answer remains and is found within these words: everything is connected. As educators, we are connected together with our passions and the sheer love of teaching. We are connected to our students in very real ways. We find joy in seeing them succeed. We are connected to the world and the people and knowledge within the world and without it. We are connected to the smallest of small and the largest of large...and we are all in it together. Learning is the process of discovering the connections that have existed for millennia and that reach far into our future as a species. Will we become Human 2.0 as Roden (2015) speculates? It is too early to know, but if advancements in science, medicine, nursing, education, and technology continue to grow exponentially as they have in the last few decades, then anything is possible! Think of the possibilities...

References

Aczel, A.D. (2002). *Entanglement: The greatest mystery in physics*. Vancouver, Canada: Raincoast.

Adler, S.L. (2014). Where is quantum theory headed? *J. Phys. Conf. Ser., 504*(012001), 1-6.

Arndt, M., & Hornberger, K. (2014). Testing the limits of quantum mechanical superpositions. *Nature Physics, 10*(4), 271-277.

Arntz, W., Chasse, B., & Vincente, M. (2006). What the bleep? Down the rabbit hole. [film]. Los Angeles, CA: Lord of the Wind Films.

Avishai-Eliner, S., Brunson, K.L., Sandman, C.A., & Baram, T.Z. (2002). Stressed out, or in (utero)? *Trends in Neurosciences, 25*(10), 519-524.

Bates, E., Thal, D., Findlay, B.L., & Clancy, B. (1995). Early language development in its neural correlates. In I. Rapin & S. Segalowitz (Eds.) *Handbook of Neuropsychology Vol 6, Child Neurology* (2nd ed.). Amsterdam: Elsevier.

Bohm, D. (1971). Quantum theory as an indication of a new order in physics. Part A: The development of new orders as shown through the history of physics. *Foundations of Physics, 1*(4), 359-384.

Bohm, D. (1973). Quantum theory as an indication of a new order in physics. B. Implicate and explicate order in physical law. *Foundations of Physics, 3*(2), 139-168.

Cohen, P. R., & Feigenbaum, E. A. (Eds.). (2014). *The handbook of artificial intelligence* (Vol. 3). Stanford, CA: Butterworth-Heinemann.

De Broglie, L. (1962). *New perspectives in physics*. New York: Basic Books.

Deng, L. (2018). Artificial intelligence in the rising wave of deep learning: The historical path and future outlook [Perspectives]. *IEEE Signal Processing Magazine, 35*(1), 180-177.

Edwards, M., Perry, B., Janzen, K., & Menzies, C. (2012). Using the artistic pedagogical technology of photovoice to promote interaction in the online post-secondary classroom: The students' perspective. *The Electronic Journal of e-Learning, 10*(1), 32-43.

Eliot, T. S. (2011). *The complete poems and plays of T.S. Eliot*. London: Faber & Faber.

Fraser, B. (2015). Classroom learning environments. In *Encyclopedia of Science Education* (pp. 154-157). Netherlands: Springer. Retrieved from https://link.springer.com/referenceworkentry/10.1007%2F978-94-007-2150-0_186

Garrison, D. R. (2016). *E-learning in the 21st century: A community of inquiry framework for research and practice*. Milton Park, UK: Taylor & Francis.

Griffiths, D.J. (2016). *Introduction to quantum mechanics*. Upper Saddle River, NJ: Prentice Hall.

Hodges, B. D. (2018). Learning from Dorothy Vaughan: Artificial intelligence and the health professions. *Medical Education, 52*(1), 11-13.

Hwang, F. (2011). *Superposition principle of wave*. Retrieved from http://www.phy.ntnu.edu.tw/ntnujava/index.php?topic=19

Parsons, J., & Taylor, L. (2011). *Student engagement: What do we know and what should we do?* Edmonton, Canada: University of Alberta. Retrieved from http://education.alberta.ca/media/6489431/student_engagement_literature_review_2011.pdf

Passanante Elman, J. (2010). After school special education: Rehabilitative television, teen citizenship, and compulsory able-bodiedness. *Television & New Media, 11*(4), 260-292.

Pollard, H., Minor, M., & Swanson, A. (2014). Instructor social presence within the community of inquiry framework and its impact on classroom community and the learning environment. *Online Journal of Distance Learning Administration, 17*(2), 1-13. Retrieved from http://citeseerx.ist.psu.edu/viewdoc/download?doi=10.1.1.849.8841&rep=rep1&type=pdf

Jammer, M. (1988). David Bohm and his work—on the occasion of his seventieth birthday. *Foundations of Physics, 18*(7), 691-699.

Janzen, K.J., MacLean, H., & Wiebe, M.A. (2016). Using online student journaling as an approach to reflection: A creative arts-based strategy. In A. Peterkin and P. Brett-MacLean (Eds.). (pp. 348-350). *Keeping reflection fresh: A practical guide for clinical educators*. Kent, OH: Kent State University Press.

Janzen, K.J., Perry, B., & Edwards, M. (2011a). Aligning the quantum perspective of learning to Instructional design: Exploring the seven definitive questions. *International Review of Research in Open and Distance Learning, 12*(7), 56-73. Retrieved from http://www.irrodl.org/index.php/irrodl

Janzen, K.J., Perry, B., & Edwards, M. (2011b). Becoming real: Using the artistic pedagogical technology of photovoice as a medium to becoming real to one another in the online educative environment. *International Journal of Nursing Education Scholarship, 8*(1), 1-17.

Janzen, K.J., Perry, B., & Edwards, M. (2012a). The entangled web: The quantum perspective of learning, quantum learning environments and Web technology. *Ubiquitous Learning: An International Journal, 4*(2), 1-17. Retrieved from http://ijq.cgpublisher.com/

Janzen, K.J., Perry, B., & Edwards, M. (2012b). Viewing Learning from a new lens: The quantum perspective of learning. *Creative Education, 3*, 712-720. Retrieved from www.scirp.org/journal/PaperInformation.aspx?PaperID=23343

Janzen, K.J., Perry, B., & Edwards, M. (2012c). Engaging students: Strategies for digital natives. *Academic Exchange Quarterly, 16*(3), 116-123. Retrieved from http://rapidintellect.com/AEQweb/cho5173.htm

Janzen, K.J., Perry, B., & Edwards, M. (2017). Engaging students: Strategies for digital natives. *Academic Exchange Quarterly, 21*(3), 70-78. [Updated version]

Janzen, K.J., Szabo, J., & Jakubec, S.L. (2016). Taking the quantum leap: Arts-based learning as a gateway into exploring transition for senior nursing students. *Journal for the Canadian Association for Curriculum Studies, 14*(1), 77-91.

King, B. F. (2018). Artificial intelligence and radiology: What will the future hold? *Journal of the American College of Radiology, 17*, 1-3.

Khrennikov, A., De Raedt, H., Plotnitsky, A., & Polyakov, S. (2015). Preface of the special issue probing the limits of quantum mechanics: Theory and experiment, Vol 1. *Foundational Physics, 45*, 707-710.

Leibniz, G. (1670/2012). *Philosophical investigations.* Retrieved from http://www.spaceandmotion.com/Philosophy-Gottfried-Leibniz-Philosopher.htm

Marquez, I. (2006). Knowledge of being v. practice of becoming in higher education: Overcoming the dichotomy in the humanities. *Arts & Humanities in Higher Education, 5*(2), 142-161.

Melrose, S., Park, C. & Perry, B. (2013). *Teaching health professionals online: Frameworks and strategies.* Edmonton, Canada: AU Press.

Merriam Webster (2018). *Entropy.* Retrieved from https://www.merriam-webster.com/dictionary/entropy

Navascués, M., Guryanova, Y., Hoban, M. J., & Acín, A. (2015). Almost quantum correlations. *Nature communications, 6*, 6288.

Onishi, T. (2018). Quantum theory. In *Quantum Computational Chemistry* (pp. 3-11). Singapore: Springer.

Parent, E. (2000). The living systems theory of James Grier Miller. Proceedings of *The First International Electronic Seminar on Wholeness.* Retrieved from http://www.isss.org/primer/asem14ep.html

Papathanasiou, I. V., Tsaras, K., & Sarafis, P. (2014). Views and perceptions of nursing students on their clinical learning environment: Teaching and learning. *Nurse Education Today, 34*(1), 57-60.

Perry, B., Edwards, M. & Janzen, K. (2014). Conceptual quilting: A medium for reflection in online courses. *eLearning Papers, 36*, 1-4.

Perry, B., Edwards, M. & Janzen, K. (2016). Haiku it!—Reflection in 17 syllables. In A. Peterkin and P. Brett-MacLean (Eds.). *Keeping reflection fresh: A practical guide for clinical educators.* (pp. 37-39). Kent, OH; Kent State University Press.

Perry, B., Janzen K.J., & Edwards, M. (2012). Enhancing online student engagement. *eLearning Papers, 30*, 1-5.

Pert, C.B. (1997). *Molecules of emotion: Why you feel the way you feel.* New York, NY: Simon & Shuster.

Pinto-Neto, N., & Struyev, W. (2018). *Bohmian quantum gravity and cosmology.* arxivpreprintArxiv.v1 1801.03353v1 [gr-qc], 1-45. Retrieved from https://arxiv.org/abs/1801.03353

Pollard, H., Minor, M. & Swanson, A. (2014). Instructor social presence within the Community of Inquiry Framework and its impact on classroom community and the learning environment. *Online Journal of Distance Learning Administration, 17*(2). Retrieved November 2, 2018 from https://www.learntechlib.org/p/152959/

Pribram, K. (2006). Holism vs. holism. *World Futures, 62*, 42-46.

Roden, D. (2015). *Posthuman life: Philosophy at the edge of the human.* London: Routledge, Taylor & Francis Group.

Siemens, G. (2006). Connectivism: Learning and knowledge today. *The International Review of Research in Open and Distance Learning, 9*(3), 1-13. Retrieved from http://admin.edna.edu.au/dspace/bitstream/2150/34771/1/gs2006_siemens.pdf

Stratford, E., Compton, L., & Wagg, F. (2017). Do we learn in utero? Does it matter? *Learning over the Life-Course: A Series of Conversations with Leon Compton,* [Media Interview] ABC Radio 936, Hobart, Tasmania, 24 October 2017, p. 2. Retrieved from http://www.abc.net.au/radio/hobart/programs/mornings/life-learning-dr-fiona-wagg/9080218

Sudbery, A. (2017). The logic of the future in quantum theory. *Synthese, 194*(11), 4429-4453.

Szabo, J., Jakubec, S.L., & Janzen, K.J. (2017). Quiet lampshade in the corner? Exploring fourth year nursing students' narratives of transition to professional practice. *Quality Advancement in Nursing Education, 2*(1), Article 4, 1-15.

Yin, J., Cao, Y., Li, Y. H., Liao, S. K., Zhang, L., Ren, J. G., ... & Li, G. B. (2017). Satellite-based entanglement distribution over 1200 kilometers. *Science, 356*(6343), 1140-1144.

Chapter 3

The Value of Creativity: Technology, Edutainment, and Play in the Classroom

In today's educational programs, there can be anywhere from 40 to 150 students in a mid to large sized class depending on the total number of students in the program. This creates challenges in not only getting to know students' names but also in carrying out learning activities with students. Artistic Pedagogical Technologies (APTs) can serve to enhance student-instructor relationships within all mediums of post-secondary learning whether it be online, hybrid, or face-to-face learning within traditional classrooms.

In larger classes, professors at times rely on teaching assistants (TAs) to lecture and assist with marking. This can further distance professors from students. The result can be a purely didactic style of teaching where the TA, or professor, becomes "the sage on the stage" rather than the "guide by the side" (King, 1993, p. 30). King emphasizes the need for revolutionary strategies to engage students in the classroom. Her seminal work, although written over 30 years ago, is still relevant today. In this age of exponential technology development and use in post-secondary classrooms, students need to rely upon more learning strategies than simply memorization. This can help students blossom in the educative environment as well as prepare them for the challenges of the workforce.

Students need to be able to articulate, access and utilize all six areas of Bloom's revised taxonomy (RBT) in terms of learning (Anderson & Krathwohl, 2001). This results in the transfer of information going beyond Bloom's lowest level of remembering, and instead reaching toward the highest level of creating (Foreman, 2010). This chapter outlines the value of edutainment and technology, and play in the classroom as a means of assisting students in reaching their peak learning potential—that of creating. Creating is discussed through the lens of APTs and examples given.

Edutainment and Technology

We all can fall into the trap of using technology for technology's sake. It's worth asking: Is it edutainment or effective technology-integrated instruction?

–Jennifer Boyle (2015)

Billsberry (2014) concludes that entertainment and education have been linked throughout the ages. As a result, the term edutainment has been used to describe this phenomenon—which really includes "two sides to the same coin" (p. 151). Corona, Cozzarelli, Palumbo and Sibilio define edutainment this way:

> The tight connection which occurs between entertainment and education has originated what is defined as edutainment which can be considered as a continuous and innovative brain-training, which stimulates, in an interactive way, the capacity to combine attention and motivation to explore and learn. (2013, p. 12)

Edutainment was first utilized in the television industry in the 1960's to educate children and adolescents (Jarvin, 2015). Since that time interest has piqued in relation to utilizing edutainment in both formal and informal teaching of adults (p. 33).

As technology has exploded and become a mainstay in the post-secondary classroom, edutainment could be considered to be reborn within the new generation of digital natives who have never known life without computerized technology (Peterson, Verenikina, & Herrington, 2008). Today's student utilizes technology ubiquitously within and without the classroom, often for the purpose of simply being entertained (Passanante Elman, 2010). This same level of entertainment is, at times, expected by students within the classroom as well.

Digital native learners may not have the skills to deal with being bored or staying focused if the material is not interesting to them. Even if course material is engaging and designed to captivate, students may distract themselves with social media and other forms of entertainment on mobile devices. The ability to multitask at times can be detrimental to students. It is questionable regarding students' ability to multitask. Probably they can only uni-task—or do one thing at a time—even if that task is minute in terms of time. How well learners multitask is debatable. This raises many questions, which at best have only partial answers, but questions which are still asked in a stance of stimulating reflection. For example, Balloffet, Courvoisier, and Lagier ask:

> Should we distinguish between places where we go to reflect [and learn] and places where we go to have fun? Should we put high[er learning] and popular culture in opposition? Should [educational] institutions be free to experiment with different forms . . . in order to be more appealing to their [students]? (2014, p. 4)

Billsberry (2014) poignantly asks if the drive behind education has become to entertain rather than to teach students. Yes, we want our classes to be interesting, and learning to be at least somewhat exciting. We wish our students would catch a fraction of the passion we feel for the field in which we teach. But is it a requirement that teachers are entertainers for this to occur? What are the associated costs of entertainment in the classroom?

Most instructors can easily tell you just how many times they have seen students on Facebook® or text messaging during classes. This speaks not only to a lack of student engagement but to the perceived need by students to be entertained or connected via the Internet and its various platforms at all times. Balloffet and colleagues (2014) refer to this as the "e-factor or entertainment factor" (p. 7). This e-factor has permeated almost all facets of our global economy (p. 7) but also has seeped into education and educational institutions. With this, we, as educators, run the risk of being tempted to provide entertainment without educative value (Peterson et al., 2008). This results in not only lost learning moments but at times lost extended learning opportunities where students could be described as lost or absent pertaining to the content teachers are attempting to share with them.

For example, one of our sons was once asked how he was doing. His reply was, "Physically present but cognitively dormant." Students can be physically present in the classroom, but cognitively dormant as well. This is similar to someone rocking in their rocking chair yet going nowhere. Facebook® in a classroom setting, when used inappropriately, is like a rocking chair. It can keep students occupied but limits their ability to learn key concepts and precludes them from adding to the group conversation or sharing personal wisdom or knowledge with the class community.

The bottom line is that educational material, if deemed as boring by students, will be ineffective (Billsberry, 2014). Ineffective learning can be detrimental not only to the student, but to post-secondary education itself. To be effective, the combination of teaching materials and teaching and learning strategies become "entertainment with a message" (p.151). Is there a level where entertainment, edutainment and education can harmoniously co-exist (Passanante Elman, 2010)? We firmly and passionately answer, "Yes!"

The integration of entertainment with a message into teaching turns the student perception that content is sterile and bland into the sense that the educational milieu is exciting, where students become eager to see what is going to happen next within the environment of the classroom. The classroom, in essence, becomes a living environment which is affected by both the professor/instructor and the student. This interaction is encapsulated by Janzen, Perry and Edwards' SITE Model (2012) which illustrates how a student, instructor, technology, and environment intersect to create engaging quantum learning environments (as outlined previously in Chapter 2).

Those students and instructors within this living-learning environment grow, develop, and learn simultaneously as each has a symbiotic relationship with the other. APTs enhance the environment, learning, and relationships, as learning (and classrooms) begin to take on a life of their own. Technology, whether big T technology (mediated by the technological explosion in today's educational world) or little t technology (using traditional mediums to promote edutainment) becomes a staple in the classroom.

An instructor need not use big T technology to engage students. APTs primarily utilize little t technology which can have big T results. This is accomplished through the use of familiar objects and mediums to interact with, and within, all aspects of holism including spiritual, emotional, cognitive, behavioral, social, corporeality, experiential, and cultural elements. Technology in the form of APTs interface with the holistic student in simple but profound ways. This can result in increased student creativity which they can then take outside the classroom and apply in their everyday lives. Knowledge, then, can become so integrated within students that there is a link created between learning, recall, and application. The adage which is attributed to Benjamin Franklin (n.d.), "Tell me and I forget. Teach me and I remember. Involve me and I learn," is enacted when APTs are part of the teaching repertoire.

APTs involve students both individually and collectively. Depending on the APT chosen for teaching a concept or idea, students' minds can be opened and new vistas can become part of the everyday classroom experience. Students can begin to anticipate what might come next in a class and can look forward to new learning experiences within the classroom. This replaces what might be perceived as dull, boring content, with learning that can enliven the senses and reach students holistically. Even online classrooms can become 'real' (Janzen, Perry & Edwards,

2011a) within the spaces of APTs, as everyday objects are utilized to enhance learning through, and within, edutainment and technology.

So, just what is the value of edutainment in terms of APTs? Students experience edutainment (education + entertainment) as they are exposed to creative arts-based strategies which link to learning, creativity and technology (Janzen, Perry & Edwards, 2017). While the term 'edutainment' has surfaced as a negative component (Billsberry, 2014), we maintain that edutainment is, and continues to, be a positive force in education.

Resnick (2004) argues against this in terms of edutainment being "things that others provide" rather than play being "things that you do" (para. 4). We propose that APTs are provided *and* are things that you do. APTs culminate in the doing and they provide mediums through which doing occurs. Thus, APTs build upon edutainment and play. When APTs are used in the classroom the benefits of APTs are realized.

Play

Play [is] a powerful learning and teaching experience.
--Janet Moyles (2014)

One of the first scholars who noted the benefits of play in children was Plato (Panksepp, 2007) who believed that children had a natural ability to play in their environment. Despite this, play consisted primarily of educational pursuits (D'Angour, 2013), In these places, called sanctuaries, children learned and grew (The Laws, VII, p. 794). Etymologically, the word sanctuary comes from the Latin *santuarium,* and denotes a place/space of a refuge or safe to be and act (Harper, 2017). For small children these sanctuaries become worlds of pure imagination and yet they remain very much grounded within their own realities. Small children spend a great deal of their time playing—whether it be toys or simple objects, other children, and/or significant others.

Play becomes part of everyday life. It is through play that children begin to master their physical, emotional, and social selves. Biologically, this change and maturation achieved through play can be seen in the development of the frontal lobe of the brain (Panksepp, 2007).

The frontal lobe of the brain basically functions in the provision of behavioral inhibition, or as Panksepp (2007) relates, this part of the brain enables us to be able to "stop, look, listen, and feel" (p. 58). Being able to do these things, leads to the ability to reflect, engage the imagination, develop empathy, and engage in creative play. Further, with as our abilities to reflect, imagine, empathize, and engage in creativity/play develop, behavioral flexibility and foresight become established as we mature and age. Bronikowska, Bronikowski, and Schott (2011) support these findings and note that "playful activity is essential for healthy development of any individual as it seems to facilitate the linkages of language, emotion, movement, socialization and cognition" (p. 24). Lieberman (2006) notes that,

> from birth to age 18, children progress from concrete to abstract thinking, from an egocentric view of events to an ability to take the other's perspective; from holding very few to holding many schemas, or mental models, about the way events occur and how social and physical environments function (p. 393).

With the abilities to think abstractly and to move beyond centration enhanced with age, one would think that humans should be able to 'play' throughout their life spans and actually spend more time playing instead of less. Biologically, play (leisure activities) in adults, is really "exposure to an enriched environment" where the environment provides "opportunities for physical activity, learning and social interaction" and results in "a host of structural and functional changes in the brain" including "the rate of neurogenesis" (Scarmeas, Lvey, Tang, Manty & Stern, 2001, p. 8).

Scarmeas and colleagues (2001) go on to note that "humans retain the capacity to generate new neurons into adulthood" and with this capacity, related to "increased brain work" in play or leisure activities, cerebral blood flow as well as glucose and oxygen metabolism is enhanced (p. 8). In view of this knowledge, playing is definitely physically beneficial for children and adults. Playing is just different as one moves from childhood into adulthood—as play becomes more complex with increased age. This complexity arises as the capacity to think and reason grows. As noted earlier, Panksepp (2007) found that the frontal brain teaches us to "stop, look, listen and feel." (p. 58). More specifically, as the frontal lobe of the brain develops, adults literally may stop playing, look at sociocultural norms for playing, listen for media messages about what is currently acceptable related to adult play (which ultimately changes from year to year), and begin to feel that natural play is only for children.

As an example, automobiles can deteriorate from the lack of use. Most notably, this could be associated with vehicles' components becoming rusty from dormancy. This can be seen with brake rotors which can become rusty in short periods of time especially in humid environments. If not used for long periods of time, this, in turn, leads to premature wear of brakes and rotors and machining or replacing become necessary

(Personal communication, M. Janzen, March 17, 2017). Relating this to playing, as individuals go through adolescence, their play skills can become rusty. The difference between rusting rotors and rusty play skills is that the spirit of play can be remembered, relearned, or revived in willing adults.

The message becomes that while children innately play, the capacity and willingness to engage in natural play as adults is often discouraged as we grow up. Forms of play such as video games/gaming, board games, or sports (in all their various formats) channel play into what has become the norm and socially acceptable for adults. While it is considered appropriate to play with a child, an adult's conception of just what constitutes play may become stifled and encroached. This is a great loss, especially in post-secondary institutions, and particularly in education. Panksepp (2007) explains this further by saying that "most... educational systems don't even recognize the value of natural play" (p. 64) even in primary educational experiences where the "dominant school culture values and expects compliance, standardization, and convergence" (Stone, 2016, p. 8). This can be partly understood in terms of social norms.

As a society, we spend a great deal of time teaching children *not* to play (i.e., quit playing with your food, stop fooling around, don't act like a kid or grow up). We as researchers believe that university students still need to play. Katherine taught three-year-olds at in an ecclesiastical setting for over three years. Some of the best lessons she used during her church pre-school classes have been successfully used with her students at the university where she is employed. She has used her ecclesiastical experiences to design her teaching activities for nursing students in the form of APTs. Let us explain.

For three-year-olds the world is a wondrous place--for many students, university is a wondrous place/space. Three-year-olds like to play--so do university students. Three-year-olds have to have activities changed up every few minutes—university students, while they have a longer attention span, need variety in learning experiences too. Three-year-olds get bored of doing the same thing over and over again-- university students likewise. Students and children both respond positively to new challenges. Three-year-olds like to create things— university students get excited when they generate something new.

Three-year-olds like stories--ditto with university students. Three-year-olds need to know that they are important to you and that you care what they think; they need to be listened to and engaged. Three-year-olds feel free to tell you when they like something or when they do not like something. Three-year-olds love to learn and apply that learning to their worlds; they like music, and playing 'pretend' (which could be understood as role play or dramatization). These things all are true of university students as well. So why not give university students opportunities to play more? Is it because we define playing so narrowly in adulthood? Can APTs become a conduit to play adult learners find appropriate and engaging and hence harness all the positive benefits of play for scholastic achievement?

As we develop from adolescence into adulthood playing becomes much more directed and focused. For adults, instead of playing holistically as children do, the play seems to become separated into distinct parts. There are unspoken rules which contravene playing in academia and "appropriate" adult play is often relegated to sports, or more recently, to games within the classroom. As mentioned before, Panksepp (2007) notes that "most ... educational systems don't even recognize the value of natural play" (p. 64). Curricula inform instructors *what* they should teach, but do not circumscribe *how* they should teach the content.

As in the Quantum Perspective of Learning (QL), if we are holistic beings with infinite capacity to learn, then it follows that we have an infinite capacity to play (Janzen, 2012). We posit that play and learning go hand in hand. Also, we suggest that playing enhances learning and every opportunity we have to play in the classroom enriches the classroom.

It may be anxiety provoking for some instructors to introduce play into their teaching approaches in they have traditionally utilized didactic lecture. However, experimentation and continued experience with teaching approaches based on play principles can lessen this anxiety. When teachers experience the positive learning outcomes of carefully crafted adult play introduced into their instruction, their anxiety about the use of play is usually lessened.

The key to the successful use of play in adult education is bringing play into the classroom and giving students permission to play once more. It is almost like we teach children not to play anymore (grow up), and then we as adult educators have to break down those barriers and teach adults that it is ok to play and even how to play. Again and again, students engaged in learning activities that some consider play say they are learning because they are having fun.

Also, it is important to recognize the link between enjoyment and learning, and creativity and learning (Janzen et al., 2017); these are inextricably entwined.

Risk-taking is part of play -- and something adults are taught to minimize or avoid. As adult teachers or adult students, we minimize risk-taking as part of our daily lives whether it be to be on neutral ground where we fit in, or as a preparatory to entering the world of employment. Taking risks, however, is part of everyday life. We take risks as we commute to work; we take risks when we take on a new project. Without taking risks, we are guaranteed not to succeed in life.

APTs can create spaces where risk-taking is done in a milieu of safety and security. APTs can create the play sanctuaries that Plato described—one's that individuals learn and grow in. In these sanctuaries students are free to just 'be' and actually have fun, explore and learn. It may resurrect memories of a happier time in education. Play at that time was a larger part of their education, compared to the oft times stressful environments of the educative classroom where much is expected of students and where the workload and program can be most demanding. Returning back to the etymology of the word sanctuary, our classrooms can become *sanctuariums* from the stresses and pressures students may feel. Learning can become fun and magical once more as students learn to play again. Learners become even more engaged as they realize that through this purposeful play they are gaining knowledge, skills and competencies that will equip them for success in their careers. (Plass et al., 2013; Resnick, 2004; Stone, 2016).

There is even a greater lack of research done with post-secondary students and play. A search of The Google Scholar database going back 10 years revealed only three articles that did not involve games, video gaming, or educational gamification (defined as seeking to add "game-like concepts to a learning process") (Glover, 2013, p. 1999). There was only a single article (Kulpa, 2017) involving post-secondary students and play as an instructional strategy. Research into other forms of play with post-secondary students provides a fertile ground for new research and understanding. Research related to the benefits of using APTs in post-secondary education can offer a link into this understanding.

Bronikowska and associates (2011) pose the question, "[Do] you think you are too old to play?" (p. 24). We posit that one is never too old to play. Play is an element of all forms of APTs: multimedia, art, sculpture, music, storytelling (narrative), poetry, drama, and a host of other mediums. APTs bring to the classroom a sense of joyful play where there are no constraints to the imagination and creativity has no (or almost limitless) bounds.

Creativity

The desire to create is one of the deepest yearnings of the human soul.

-- Dieter F. Uchtdorf (2008)

The desire to create has fueled humankind for untold millennia. Creativity has brought us from the making of fire and cave drawings to newly conceived technology for our future that defies the imagination. Our own words—think of the possibilities—has become one of several mantras for us as we have explored using APTs in our own (and others') classrooms. We, as a research team, are carrying out research through a national four-year grant to substantiate the theory behind APTs (which was delineated in Chapter Two). The past 13 years of research on APTs (see Chapter Five) lends much support to the conclusion that APTs *do* positively affect the development of critical thinking and creativity skills of graduate and undergraduate nursing-students.

In searching the literature, it becomes evident that games/gaming have been the most studied of all types of adult play due to their multiple benefits (Cornona et al., 2013; Glover, 2013; Granic, Lobel & Engles, 2014; Kulpa, 2017). There is a paucity of literature or research on the benefits of play in forums/formats other than in the disciplines of mathematics and science. We have found play enhances a myriad of factors in the post-secondary classroom and can absolutely assist instructors and students in stimulating creativity (Janzen et al., 2017).

There is much support in the literature pertaining to the need for, and benefits of, creativity in all classrooms from primary to graduate levels (Chan, 2012; Duhamel, 2016; Jarvin, 2015; Ramma, Samy, & Gopee, 2015; Stone, 2016; Turner & Wattanakul, 2016). Further, this is well reflected in literature surrounding creativity in nursing education. For example, Mitchell and Hall (2007) used creativity as an approach to teaching spirituality to midwives. MacDonnell and MacDonald (2011) employed guided imagery, images, narrations and poetry to facilitate creative, critical inquiry in nursing. Through Chan's (2012) and Duhamel's (2016) literature reviews related to nurturing creativity in nursing education, it appears that creativity—especially those strategies utilizing creative arts—have been used extensively in nursing education over the past decade.

There are varied definitions of creativity. Tsai (2015) defines creativity, in terms of education, as a pedagogical approach saying,

> Creativity is presented as a means, not an end; it is the use of creative methods to promote students' learning. In this sense,

creative education can be broadly defined as creative ways of teaching, thinking, and learning. (p. 158)

To be creative is to view situations differently from the norm and to act upon those situations in spontaneous ways. Creativity generates thought(s), feeling(s), or product(s) inside or outside oneself or others. Creativity can inspire others to create.

Although Sopoci, Larson, Rugh and Tait (2016) state that "necessity fuels creativity" (p. 94), we believe that creativity fuels creativity. The more opportunities that students are given to be creative, the more creative they can be. This begins (as with play) with giving permission to students to explore their own creativity through class activities such as APTs. Play puts students in a position of vulnerability. When what students create and share is appreciated and acknowledged by the instructor and/or class members, trust is gained and students are more likely to continue to be open and to continue to create. For example, in dating relationships, individuals are vulnerable when they share an idea or a thought with others. When something is shared, and what is shared is positively/respectfully received, trust is perpetuated, and the individual is willing to share more. Through repeated experiences like this, the relationship can grow and develop into deeper layers of trust.

Learning is enhanced in situations of vulnerability and trust. There is a certain vulnerability in learning something new. We learn as we seek knowledge and skills we do not have. This is true of instructors as well, as instructors also learn from their students. The more creativity that an instructor can infuse into a course, the more the instructor potentially learns too. This, of course, involves vulnerability on the part of the instructor. The linking of vulnerability and trust has ties to what I term as free creativity.

Free creativity is the process of creativity where there is nothing driving the desire to create other than creation itself. The more individuals engage in free creativity, the better they become in demonstrating creativity. Hence creativity, fueled by creativity experiences, develops and grows over time with use.

For example, children engage in free creativity as they free play. A blanket over two chairs may become a castle. Guitar players may engage in free creativity as they sit playing the guitar in what is commonly termed just fooling around; experimenting with the instrument's melodies and harmonies. Hockey players playing an impromptu game of street hockey may try out some new moves thus engaging in free creativity. Thus, in these unconstrained activities, free creativity becomes a creative process which can be enhanced through time and experiences.

It is well documented that play fosters creativity (Boyle, 2015; Liberman, 2006; Stone, 2016). While Plato described and promoted creativity as a measure of inspiration, Kant attributed creativity to imagination (Gaut, 2010). We believe that every student and instructor possesses a measure of inspiration; imagination which culminates in creativity.

Creativity helps generate multiple layers of association which can promote long-term memories or retention of things learned. Creativity engages the visual, the kinesthetic, the hands-on, and the auditory. For example, elementary through secondary school students enjoy science fairs in part because they get to create. Creation requires learners to put into practice what they are learning. This using theory to fuel practice can be evident in individual and/or group projects in classes.

Further, creativity can have the effect of bringing forward material used in previous, concurrent, and future classes. In traditional learning environments, students may only look at the course material with tunnel vision. The common experience students report is memorizing content for the summative exam and then filing the knowledge away to be retrieved (hopefully) when needed. Creative environments encourage students to apply learnings in multiple ways, to work with (and use) acquired knowledge as it is acquired, and even to escape the boundaries of the course and connect what they have learned to other learning experiences in the outside world.

Where playing is an accepted and anticipated part of the instruction, creativity can become the hallmark of edutainment, technology, and play. Where we construct play sanctuaries in classrooms, permission is granted and learners are invited to be creative. To us, there is no greater example of a creative teacher, than that of teacher Miss Frizzle from Scholastics' "The Magic School Bus" television series.

"The Magic School Bus" television series ran from 1994-1999 with the main character Miss Frizzle—an "eccentric" school teacher who could be described as the teacher everyone would want to have (Coyle & Degan, 1994, para. 1). Miss Frizzle's mantra, "Take chances, make mistakes, get messy!" (para. 7), has become another mantra (and we hope with our students) within our own nursing theory classrooms. As we explain this to students, and as we explain the use and reasoning behind using APTs, the students all smile and some of them laugh as they remember Miss Frizzle.

Like Miss Frizzle, it is my goal to take students on 'adventures in playing' within the classroom and to promote creativity within each student. In

Miss Frizzle's class, the whole was greater than the sum of the parts. It took the strengths of all of the students to achieve the end result. Learning in this way was inclusive for all members of the class. This, we believe, begins with modeling creativity as an instructor. Let us share an example.

Theory classes are started each semester with a five-minute digital photostory (complete with background music) to introduce ourselves to the students. This past semester all students clapped when the digital photo story, entitled, "The Adventure," finished. Their delight was palpable and hence not only play (in the form of APTs) but also creativity (through our example) was introduced into the third year theory class on Seniors Health. APTs continued to be used throughout this six-week intensive course to help engage learners and to drive the learning benefits of this pedagogical approach. Creativity is part of this course from the first moments of the first class. Risks are taken and vulnerability demonstrated by doing something unorthodox in the introduction. Through this approach, learners are shown expectations and we demonstrate that they have permission to be creative in their assignments and interactions. APTs give students opportunities to be creative during this class. As Resnick (2004) explains, and we concur, (emphatically we might add), my "ultimate [goal] is a world full of playfully creative [nurses], who are constantly inventing new opportunities for themselves" (p. 4), their patients, and the environments they work in. Through this creativity, innovation is fostered.

Through innovation, the world of healthcare is changed, shaped, and molded into a better place—for all involved within a student nurse's sphere of influence. That difference ultimately begins with creativity in their approaches to solving human and technological challenges. This makes nurses more human, and more humane, in a healthcare world often driven by big T technology.

Technology can further be described as hard technology or soft technology (Dron, 2011). Siu and Wong (2015) purport that both hard and soft technologies are requisite in education. In nursing, hard technology is often associated with machine-like technology and processes, while soft technology is more associated with human factors such as touch, caring, and the expression of compassion. Dron reminds us that "soft technologies are flexible, supporting creativity and change, because the gaps inside them have to be filled with processes constructed by people" (para. 5).

There are gaps in the educational process as well as in health care processes. This can be seen in the theory-practice gap where students do not or cannot connect theory to practice. It is not enough to merely 'know' in education, but rather it is imperative that students 'understand.' Westin,

Sundler, and Berglund (2015) support this statement, "in the field of nursing, learning has shifted from 'doing' to 'understanding'" (p. 1). Effective nurses cannot function by rote memory or by memorizing procedures, they must think critically and creatively and be willing and able to innovate to meet client needs optimally.

Part of the filling this gap can begin in theory classes where this gap-filling involves the use of APTs. APTs become the mortar of innovation that binds learning, change, and creativity together. The outcome is that APTs help students understand nursing in a richer, deeper way. APTs are flexible and can be adapted to fit any curriculum in nursing, or other discipline. This flexibility can translate into the use of APTs in almost all courses and beyond. This includes practicums, and in face-to-face, hybrid or online delivery formats. In Chapter Four, 35 APTs are presented that illustrate these propositions.

References

Anderson, L.W., & Krathwohl, D.R. (Eds.) (2001). *A taxonomy for learning, teaching and assessing: A revision of Bloom's taxonomy of educational objectives.* New York: Longman.

Arndt, M., & Hornberger, K. (2014). Testing the limits of quantum mechanical superpositions. *Nature Physics, 10*(4), 271.

Balloffet, P., Courvoisier, F. H., & Lagier, J. (2014). From museum to amusement park: The opportunities and risks of edutainment. *International Journal of Arts Management, 16*(2), 4-17.

Belchior, P., Marsiske, M., Leite, W. L., Yam, A., Thomas, K., & Mann, W. (2016). Older adults' engagement during an intervention involving off-the-shelf videogame. *Games for Health Journal, 5*(3), 151-156.

Billsberry, J. (2014). The rise and rise of management edutainment. *Journal of Management Education, 38*(2), 151-159.

Boyle, J. (2015). Edutainment or effective technology integration? *Reading Today, 32*(4), 28-30. Retrieved from http://www.literacy2pointzero.com/download/IRA-EdTech-Article-Jennifer-Boyle.pdf

Bronikowska, M., Bronikowski, M., & Schott, N. (2011). "You think you are too old to play?" Playing games and aging. *Human Movement, 12*(1), 24-30.

Chan, Z.C.Y. (2012). A systematic review of creative thinking/creativity in nursing education. *Nursing Education Today.* Retrieved from htpp://dx.doi.org/1010.16/j.nedt.2012.09.005

Corona, F., Cozzarelli, C., Palumbo, C., & Sibilio, M. (2013). Information technology and edutainment: Education and entertainment in the age of interactivity. *International Journal of Digital Literacy and Digital Competence (IJDLDC), 4*(1), 12-18.

Coyle, C., & Degan, B. (Creators) (1994). The magic school bus. [Television]. Retrieved from http://www.imdb.com/title/tt0108847/

D'Angour, A. (2013). Plato and play: Taking education seriously in ancient Greece. *American Journal of Play, 5*(3), 293-307.

Dron, J. (2011). The nature of technologies. Retrieved from http://change.mooc.ca/post/367

Duhamel, K.V. (2016). Bringing us back to our creative senses: Fostering creativity in graduate-level nursing education: A literary review. *Nurse Education Today, 45*, 51-54. Retrieved from http://dx.doi.org/10.1016/j.nedt.2016.06.016

Forehand, M. (2010). Bloom's taxonomy. *Emerging perspectives on learning, teaching, and technology, 41*, 47. Retrieved from htttp://projects.coe.uga.edu/epltt/index.php?title=Bloom's_Taxonomy

Franklin, B. (n.d.) BrainyQuote.com. Retrieved from https://www.brainyquote.com/quotes/quotes/b/benjaminfr383997.html

Gaut, B. (2010). The philosophy of creativity. *Philosophy Compass, 5*(12), 1034-1046. Retrieved from http://cjfraser.net/site/uploads/2014/08/The-Philosophy-of-CreativityGaut.pdf

Glover, I. (2013). Play as you learn: Gamification as a technique for motivating learners. In J. Herrington, A. Couros, & V. Irvine (Eds.). Proceedings of the World Conference on Educational Multimedia and Telecommunications 2013. Chesapeake, VA. AACE, 1999-2008.

Granic, I., Lobel, A., & Rutger, C.M.E. (2014). The benefits of playing video games. *American Psychologist, 69*(1), 66-78.

Harper, D. (2017) Sanctuary. *Etymology Dictionary Online*. Retrieved from http://www.etymonline.com/index.php?allowed_in_frame=0&search=sanctuary

Janzen, K.J., Perry, B., & Edwards, M. (2011). Becoming real: Using the artistic pedagogical technology of photovoice as a medium to becoming real to one another in the online educative environment. *International Journal of Nursing Education Scholarship, 8*(1), Article 6, 1-17. doi: https://doi.org/10.2202/1548-923X.2168,

Janzen, K.J., Perry, B., & Edwards, M. (2012). The entangled web: The quantum perspective of learning, quantum learning environments and web technology. *Ubiquitous Learning: An International Journal, 4*(2), 1-15.

Janzen, K.J., Perry, B., & Edwards (2017). Building blocks: Enmeshing technology and creativity with artistic pedagogical technologies. *Turkish Online Journal of Distance Education, 18*(1), 4-21.

Jarvin, L. (2015). Edutainment, games, and the future of education in a digital world. In E. L. Grigorenko (Ed.), *New Directions for Child and Adolescent Development, 147*, 33–40. doi: 10.1002/cad.20082

King, A. (1993). From sage on the stage to guide on the side. *College teaching, 41*(1), 30-35.

Kulpa, A. (2017). Applied gamification: Reframing evaluation in post-secondary classrooms. *College Teaching*. Retrieved from http://dxdoi.org/10.1080/87567555.2016.1232693

Lieberman, D.A. (2006). What can we learn from playing interactive games? In P. Vorderer & J. Bryant (Eds.), *Playing video games: Motives, responses, and consequences.* (pp. 379-397). Mahwah, NJ: Lawrence Erlbaum Associates.

MacDonnell, J.A., & MacDonald, G. (2011). Arts-based critical inquiry in nursing and interdisciplinary professional education: Guided imagery, images, narratives, and poetry. *Journal of Transformative Education, 9*(4), 203-221.

Mitchell, M., & Hall, J. (2007). Teaching spirituality to student midwives: A creative approach. *Nursing Education in Practice, 7*, 416-424. http://dx.doi.org/10.1016/j.nepr.2007.02.007

Moyles, J. (2014). *The excellence of play.* New York: University Press.

Panksepp, J. (2007). Can PLAY diminish ADHD and facilitate the construction of the social brain? *Journal of Canadian Academy of Child Adolescent Psychiatry, 16*(2), 57–66.

Passanante Elman, J. (2010). After school special education: Rehabilitative television, teen citizenship, and compulsory able-bodiedness. *Television & New Media, 11*(4), 260-292.

Peterson, R., Verenikina, I., & Herrington, J. (2008). *Standards for educational, edutainment, and developmentally beneficial computer games.* Retrieved from http://ro.uow.edu.au/cgi/viewcontent.cgi?article=1063&context=edupapers

Plass, J. L., O'Keefe, P. A., Homer, B. D., Case, J., Hayward, E. O., Stein, M., & Perlin, K. (2013). The impact of individual, competitive, and collaborative mathematics game play on learning, performance, and motivation. *Journal of Educational Psychology, 105*(4), 1050-1066.

Ramma, Y., Samy M., & Gopee, A. (2015). Creativity and innovation in science and technology: Bridging the gaps between secondary and tertiary levels of education. *International Journal of Education Management, 29*(1), 2-17.

Resnick, M. (2004). Edutainment? No thanks. I prefer playful learning. *Associazione Civita Report on Edutainment, 14*, 1-4. Retrieved from https://llk.media.mit.edu/papers/edutainment.pdf

Scarmeas, N., Levy, G., Tang, M.X., & Manly, J., & Stern, Y. (2001). Incidence of leisure activity on the incidence of Alzheimer's disease. *Neurology 26*(57), 2236-2242.

Siu, K. W. M., & Wong, Y. L. (2015). Soft and hard technologies in technology education. In *Curriculum design and classroom management: Concepts, methodologies, tools, and applications*, (pp. 378-391). Hershey, PA: IGI Global.

Scopoci, K., Larson, E., Rugh, R., & Tait, B. (2016). Necessity fuels creativity: Adapting long- distance collaborative methods for the classroom. *Journal of Dance Education, 16*(3), 94-98. Retrieved from http://dx.doi.org.10.1080/15290824.2016.1198010

Stone, B. (2016). Playing around in science: How self-directed inquiry benefits the whole child. *International Journal of the Whole Child, 1*(1), 1-10. Retrieved from http://libjournals.mtsu.edu/index.php/ijwc/article/viewFile/599/544

Tsai, K.C. (2015). A framework of creative education. *In Education, 21*(1), 137-155. Retrieved from http://ineducation.ca/ineducation/article/view/193/733

Turner, K., & Wattanakul, B. (2016). Development of ERC IF model to increase critical thinking and creativity skills of undergraduate nursing students. *International Journal of Science, Behavioral, Educational, Economic, Business and Industrial Engineering, 10*(6), 1884- 1889. Retrieved from http://waset.org/publications/10004641/

Uchtdorf, D.F. (2008). Happiness, your heritage. Retrieved from https://www.lds.org/general-conference/2008/10/happiness-your-heritage?lang=eng

Westin, L., Sundler, A. J., & Berglund, M. (2015). Students' experiences of learning in relation to didactic strategies during the first year of a nursing programme: A qualitative study. *BMC Medical Education, 15*(1), 1-8.

Chapter 4

Artistic Pedagogical Technologies: 35 Examples

Since 2006 when APTs were first envisioned by Beth, there has been quite an expansion in the number of APTs available for use in the face-to-face, blended, and online learning environments. From a single APT to now over 35 APTs, APTs can become a staple in the nursing classroom. With one or two APTs used in each class over the semester, students can learn to look forward to APTs as part of their regular learning experience. In this chapter, examples of 35 APTs are presented with accompanying instructions for use and any adaptations for online, blended, or face-to-face learning environments.

1. Photovoice

Photovoice was originally presented by Wang and Burris (1997) as a tool for action participatory research. Beth envisioned a revised form of Photovoice (PV) the research methodology that became PV the teaching strategy (Perry, 2006). As a research approach, PV focused on engaging research participants in telling their stories using photographic images. The idea that images convey meaning seemed equally applicable to learning as students need ways (other than written text) to share their beliefs and knowledge with classmates and instructors. PV the teaching strategy was at first quite rudimentary as Beth posted a digital image in an online graduate course on change management and asked learners to comment on what they saw in the image that helped explain change theory. The response was overwhelmingly positive. The image seemed to capture students' interest and learners quickly posted links between theory and what they saw in the photo. Class discussion resulted as learners compared their analysis of theory and the image. The depth of analysis and amount of interaction was remarkable. PV the teaching strategy was refined and became an approach used in many courses for several purposes.

Here is how PV works. A photographic image (chosen by the instructor) is displayed with an accompanying reflective question. Students are invited to respond to the question with the image in mind. This activity can be used in face-to-face, blended, and online learning environments. An example of a PV that we have used is an image of a butterfly going through the last transition of metamorphosis. An accompanying reflective question could be "How is your transition from fourth-year nursing student to new graduate like this image?"

Figure 4.1 Modsell (2012)

This APT can be used in online, face-to-face, and blended classrooms. PV can be used to introduce weekly topics or concepts, as a reflective tool for summarizing concepts, or as a single PV in some aspect of course work. In the online learning environment, the PV image is posted in a separate forum that students can reply to. Other students are invited to provide feedback to their classmates' posts. Instructors also comment, although usually at the end of the discussion period so as not to influence student views. In face-to-face learning environments, the image can be posted as part of a PowerPoint™ presentation with an accompanying question. Students can be given the option of typing or handwriting their responses for the instructor who then provides feedback to individual students focused on their analysis of the image.

2. Conceptual Quilting

Conceptual Quilting (Perry & Edwards, 2009) is an electronic form of quilting where students use software of their choice to create multiple quilt squares and form these into a digital quilt. Learners are directed to create individual quilt squares that represent "concepts, theories, ideas, and metaphors in the course [that] made an impression on [them] (p. 190) during the course. In this way, it is a reflection activity as students focus on what they take away for the course at the conclusion of the class. Creating the conceptual quilt necessitates that learners review the course materials to locate the ideas they will focus on in their quilts. Quilt making is an engaging way to encourage students to review and reflect. Creating a quilt also forces learners to hone in on key ideas that they will take forward with them in their further learning. Upon completion of all student quilts, the quilts are placed in a virtual 'quilt gallery.' All class members "walk" through the online quilt gallery, look at their classmates' quilts, and make comments and observations on a discussion board. This quilting activity can be utilized in online or blended courses. This APT can act to bring closure to an online course in which students may have developed strong relationships with their fellow students. (See Figure 4.2)

Figure 4.2 (Haler, 2010; Perry, 2018)

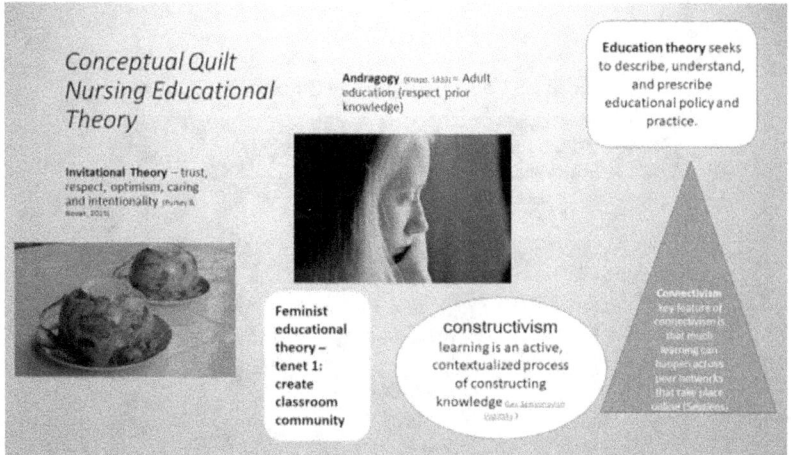

3. Collective Quilting

Collective Quilting (Janzen, 2013) is a derivative of Conceptual Quilting and created especially for use in face-face learning environments. This activity is used as the capstone activity in the final class of the semester. Each student (and the instructor) chooses one four by four-inch quilt square. The squares come in a variety of colors and patterns. Each quilt square has a sticky label that participants can write on. The instructor prepares the blank quilt squares beforehand. Students are asked to write down what they are going to take away from the course. This could be a concept, a class that the student enjoyed the most, or an overarching highlight from the course.

Upon completion of the individual quilt squares, students are invited to come to a space in the classroom (usually the front of the classroom) and lay their quilt squares down on the floor. The first student then speaks to what he/she wrote on the quilt square. Following this, students take turns laying their squares and speaking to what their squares mean to them. Gradually a quilt is formed.

When all quilt squares are on the floor, the instructor lays his/her quilt square and speaks to the class regarding the square. Usually, the instructor relates what he/she will remember most about that particular class or what made teaching that class memorable. When students are dismissed, the instructor can take the quilt and reflect upon individual squares and themes. As a summative tool, this can help the instructor to realize what aspect(s) of his/her teaching stood out most in that class. As with Conceptual Quilting, this can, in the face-to-face learning environment, act to give closure to a course where relationships may have been forged. (See Image 4.3)

Figure 4.3 Collective Quilting (Janzen, 2017)

4. Virtual Reflective Centers

Virtual Reflective Centers (VRCs) (Perry & Edwards, 2009) are an online or blended classroom tool to encourage reflection and interactional questioning. VRCs take the form of role playing in terms of motivational interviewing. VRCs were originally created for face-face-classrooms, and further developed for the online learning environment by Cubbon (Personal communication November 12, 2007). VRCs have benefits of simulation learning in a safe environment. This activity is undertaken in a chat room and recorded. Students have an assigned role (nurse, patient, etc.), they each get a script (private), and then they meet at an assigned time and role play a scene based on their script. Students use audio and video during their role play and learners can record their sessions for sharing with classmates, for themselves to review later, or for instructors for review and grade if it is a marked activity.

The VRC should not take longer than 15 minutes. Students can then post their interactions for the instructor and classmates if this is how the instructor has planned to use the VRCs. This sharing promotes teambuilding and students have the opportunity to learn by watching what others did well (or not so well). VRCs are essentially inexpensive and easy forms of simulation.

VRCs can be adapted to a variety of classroom topics or situations, for example learning to: communicate with older adult patients; conduct a suicide-risk assessment with a client; or complete a pre-op patient history form. The VRC can be adapted to face-to-face learning environments by utilizing mobile devices to video-record students' interviews and then posting them to an online forum created for this purpose.

5. The Great Debate

The Great Debate has several forms that can be undertaken depending on which learning environment the instructor is in. In the online and blended environments, students are given a topic and asked to take the "side of the debate that is contrary to their own current beliefs on the topic" (Perry & Edwards, 2009, p. 189). The students each prepare a presentation in the form of a PowerPoint™ presentation and post it to a dedicated online forum. Students use the balance of a specific week to debate the topic in the forum. For example, a topic could be, "nurses should advocate for the development of safe-injection sites for illicit drug users."

Variations on the Great Debate include the 'One Minute Self-Debate' which has students work alone and debate a resolution independently. For example, in a class for second-year students (Theoretical Foundation), there is a section on compassion fatigue. Students are given the article,

Against Compassion: Understanding Institutional Perfidy as Evil, by Wendy Austin (2011) as pre-reading, and then given a resolution such as, "Be it resolved that healthcare institutions are responsible for compassion fatigue in nurses." Students then follow the process for the One Minute Self-Debate which includes:

i. Agree with the resolution and write down one point for your side of the resolution.
ii. Disagree with the resolution and write down one point for your other side (the negative).
iii. Rebut yourself. Any heated self-discussions?
iv. Share your finest point on the conference forum.

6. Point-Counter Point Reflection

In the point-counterpoint reflection activity, students are given two opposite perspectives for consideration. Students then write a reflection based on the perspective that most closely follows their own value/belief system. Point-counterpoint reflections can be utilized in all three learning environments. For blended or online learning environments, the choice of perspective and the students' reflections can be posted on an online forum. In face-to-face classrooms, students can write/type a reflection and hand it in or email it to their instructor for feedback.

As an example of a point-counterpoint reflection, students could be asked to consider two opposite viewpoints on caring.

a. Point – Caring is a learned behavior.
b. Counterpoint – Caring is an innate behavior.

Question - Which argument holds most closely to your belief system and why? Present your reflection to the class.

There may be background reading included in the course that would be useful to students participating in the point-counterpoint activity. This reading is completed before students participate in the exercise.

7. Mission Impossible

In the face-to-face learning environment, The Great Debate activity can be used as the foundation for a variation exercise called 'Mission Impossible.' Students are divided into two groups according to the last letter of their surnames (e.g., A to M and N to Z) and each group is asked to debate a topic of the instructor's choice. Students are given 20 minutes to prepare for the debate and the actual debate takes no longer than 15 minutes. The instructor acts as an intermediary between the two groups.

For example, in a class on leadership, the instructor prepares a "mission" for students which could be likened to the movie "Mission Impossible"(De Palma, 1996). The instructor plays the YouTube™ of the theme song for the movie while handing out envelopes to each group. These envelopes contain the group's "mission." Specifically, the groups have the mission of debating whether Tinkerbell or Captain Hook would make a better leader. Students must justify their choice using theories and ideas from the leadership course. Besides the mission, a picture of each character is included in the envelopes handed out to students.

A series of nesting envelopes are used to increase excitement and anticipation. The envelopes include:

1. The outside envelope that says "Mission Impossible."
2. A second envelope (inside the first) that mimics the way Ethan Hawkes (the main character in the series of movies) receives his missions. "Your mission—if you choose to accept it—This will self-destruct in 30 seconds" (De Palma, 1996).
3. A final envelope (inside the second envelope) that gives students their mission.

Students are instructed to use everything that they have learned during the course on leadership to debate their position. In the years of using this APT, students have a great deal of fun as they prepare for and debate their position. Course content is applied during the debate. Both sides are declared "winners" in this impossible debate as there are no right or wrong answers. This activity can be adapted for use in online or blended classrooms.

8. Poetic Learning Activities

Poetic Learning includes a set of APTs that can creatively engage students and encourage reflection on course themes. Learners from face-to-face, blended, and online learning environments can equally participate in poetry-based APTs. In blended and online courses, poems can be posted in an online forum for a "virtual poetry reading" (Perry, Janzen & Edwards, 2011, p. 2). In face-to-face courses, the instructor can either invite students to share poetry about a course theme in class or ask students to hand their poems in for feedback. These poems can be either composed by students themselves or sourced by the students from published poetry. There are three main types of poetry-based APTs: reflective poetry, parallel poetry, and Haiku-It!

In reflective poetry, students are invited to write poems after thinking about course content or about cases the instructor has given the class.

Other times, instructors give students existing poems related to class themes and use these as the foundation for class discussions. For example, in a second-year theory class on ethics students were told about Katherine, as a new graduate nurse, who was caring for an elderly man whose amputation had become infected. Katherine performed dressing changes on the man twice a day. The patient badly needed a revision of his amputation, but the man's son and the surgeon had argued, and subsequently, the surgeon refused to do the revision. Katherine had written a poem about her experience with this patient entitled *Moral Distress*. This poem became a springboard for class discussion on the broader topic of solving ethical dilemmas.

Moral Distress

I stood at the door of his room.
He lay there
Quiet
And just stared out the window.
He never looked at me
As I told him
It was time for his dressing change.

As I prepared my sterile field
And opened boxes and boxes of gauze
I took a deep breath;
Telling him I would take the old dressing off
And then clean his wound.
I knew it was my duty.
Despite the Morphine
He screamed in agony
And screamed again each time
I touched his wound.
I wore a mask
As the odor coming from the wound
Was putrid.

The mask that day
Covered more than the odor.
It covered my tears
As I silently wept.

> I knew it was my duty
> to do something to help this screaming man
> In so much pain...
> But what?
> I was only a new grad
> Just out of training.
> Would anyone listen to me?

To initiate the class discussion, students were invited to finish the last stanza of Katherine's poem. After sharing their thoughts in this form, a rich conversation was led by the instructor.

Reflective poetry APT can be adapted for use in online, face-to-face, and blended learning environments. In online and blended courses, the students can post the stanza they compose for an instructor provided poem in an online forum. In face-to-face courses, the last stanza can be shared by each student with classmates.

9. Parallel Poetry

In Parallel Poetry, the instructor writes (or chooses a poem from published poetry) and posts the poem for the class. Students are invited to write a poem of their own which is similar in "topic, rhythm, form, and cadence" (Perry et al., 2011, p. 2) to the initial poem. To adapt this to a face-to-face learning environment, students can be presented with the poem on a PowerPoint™ or other presentation forum and asked to write a poem that is parallel to the one the instructor has presented. The resultant poems can be shared orally in face-to-face classes or posted to a site such as Blackboard™ or Moodle™ in online courses.

The following poems illustrate parallel poetry.

Instructor Poem

The Abyss

> There are times
> Patients find themselves
> On the edge of the abyss.
> On the verge
> Of losing hope
> And fearing abandonment.
> They reach toward us...their nurses.

In moments of
Pain, anguish or fear
We reach back
Only as we know how.
Our words, our actions,
Our very presence—
Communicates our promise
That we will never abandon.

At all times—
Even after death's passing
We stand with
Families...
Infusing them with
Our strength
Our courage
Our hope. (Janzen & Perry, 2014)

Student Poem

The Ravine

There are times
When patients are caught in the ravine
Cold, hungry, destitute, and in despair.
We as nurses, reach out our hands to them.

They reach upward with feeble hands
And take our hands:
Warm, comforting, and strong
And we help pull them out.
Always with the promise
That we will never abandon.

For nurses are there for the duration...
To the very end
Together we are stronger;
Together life holds promise
As our courage, faith, and hope
Combine as one.

Some students find writing poetry a challenge. However, parallel poetry provides would-be writers a template or format to follow making this activity easier. Beyond writing of poetry, students must grasp the concepts, attitudes, and nuances reflected in the instructors' poem in order to be able to develop and shape the content of their parallel poem. Parallel poetry demonstrates achievement of higher-order learning outcomes.

10. Haiku-It!

Haiku-It! Uses Haiku, a Japanese form of poetry that has 17 syllables. The first line of a Haiku has five syllables, the second seven, and the third and final line has five syllables. This type of poetry challenges students to be concise in their writing. To be concise, they must first develop a clear understanding of the content they wish to convey.

Haiku-It! can be used in all learning environments to summarize a concept, course reading, course discussion, or course theme. An example of Haiku-It! poetry to explain the course concept of managing conflict follows:

Conflict

Anger yet prevails
Loud, yet imperceptible
In battle, both lose.

Haikus can be written by students and then shared with class colleagues to trigger class discussion and further insights about a course topic. Haikus are also useful as the concluding activity for a course, a final challenge as students are asked to distill the course in 17 memorable syllables.

11. Minute at the Movies

This APT utilizes a movie trailer or a clip from a movie (available on YouTube™) that is related to a course topic. Students view the trailer or clip and then are provided with questions that assist them in reflection about the topic being demonstrated. For example, a movie trailer from the Disney movie, *Brave* (Andrews, Chapman & Purcell, 2012) depicts an Irish princess who demonstrates bravery in the face of danger. This APT using *Brave* can be useful in a unit which focuses on the concept of safety as it acts as an impetus for class discussion about being honest regarding medication or other errors made while in clinical. Another example is a clip from the movie *Green Fried Tomatoes* (Avenet, 1991) in which Ruth (one of the main characters) is dying, and her best friend Idgy is by her side. This clip, along with reflective questions provided by the instructor, can allow students to focus on the roles of nurses and others in providing palliative care.

12. Our Community Soap Scenes

Our Community Soap Scenes combines the drama of a soap opera with Facebook™-like profiles to stimulate reflection and help students to reach higher-order cognitive and affective domain learning outcomes. The instructor develops several soap opera character profiles prior to the beginning of a course. These characters are members of an imagined community of the instructor's choosing. For example, if a course theme relates to the health of homeless people living in a large city the profiles could be various members of this community (police, drug abusers, prostitute, community nurse, etc.), and the setting or community could be downtown Edmonton. Throughout the course, members of the fictious community are featured in scenarios, each of which focuses on a course concept. These stories are presented featuring individuals profiled initially, and the class discusses each situation.

Further, as the course progresses, attributes and actions of individual fictitious community members can be integrated into other course discussions. The individuals who are characters developed in the profiles at the outset of the course become "real" to the students in the class and they can be used as examples and to illustrate points made during class discussions throughout the course. Blank profile templates are provided so that students can create additional community members as the course progresses. Students who choose to can also add to profiles of themselves to the collection of community members as the course progresses.

13. Theme Songs

Theme Songs is an APT that uses music. Theme Songs can be used to aid learning in all learning environments. The benefits of utilizing a theme song are found within the music itself. Specifically, "Music evokes emotion, and a theme song (used strategically during the course) may provide learners with a community-building commonality" (Perry et al., 2011, p. 3).

Choosing a theme song can be a difficult decision for instructors as class members may enjoy different genres of music. Instrumental songs can be an appropriate choice as songs with lyrics may be distracting or offensive. It may be more effective to have students choose the class theme song as a group or to have a rotating theme song with students taking turns choosing the theme for a week (or a day). Royalty free online sites such as www.jamendo.com provide instructors (or students) with the opportunity to choose a song. Course theme songs can have positive outcomes such as fostering team-building (classmates working together to choose a course theme song), helping learners get to know one another (if they each choose a song for the course that appeals to them), and helping with retention of knowledge (e.g., whenever class participants hear "their" song they will all think of that specific course and the course content). An example of a theme song, *Destiny*, was used in a graduate course. This song was chosen by the instructor and offered to students at the beginning of each unit of the course (and at stressful times throughout the course such as when students were about to write an exam). *Destiny* was located on the website Jamendo and has a creative commons license for use for educational purposes (Perry et al., 2011). Theme music is an APT that is suitable for online, blended, and face-to-face learning environments.

14. Story-telling

For centuries, story-telling has been a staple for passing on oral traditions as well as for providing knowledge and entertainment. Sharing stories with nursing students assists in bringing concepts to life. Students can relate to these stories (narratives) as they begin to have experiences in clinical which relate to the stories. Stories can engage learners by creating an atmosphere of anticipation and inviting involvement. When instructors share their own nursing stories, students begin to view their teachers as 'real' persons. This is especially helpful in online learning environments when students may feel isolated and distanced from their teachers. Teaching presence is created as students learn about instructors from situations they have faced in their nursing careers. Story-telling can be used in the online, blended, and face-to-face learning environments.

15. Story Writing

Like story-telling, story writing helps students to articulate their clinical (and other experiences) in enhanced detail. When students write about an encounter they have had during a clinical placement they may explore the affective aspect of that experience. Students choose the medium they prefer to use to capture their stories: pen and paper format, online in a document, or posted to an online forum. The variety of possibilities for formats makes stories easily adaptive to any learning environment. Students can subsequently share their stories with instructors or with their classmates by presenting them orally in a face-to-face class or by posting them online. Student stories can vary in length, but one to two pages is usually sufficient for students to recount enough details of a situation for analysis to be possible.

16. Word Sculptures

Working with various mediums, students can create word sculptures to illustrate single concepts, solidify learning about a series of ideas, or as a method for capturing and organizing key points from a lecture. In the face-to-to face learning environment crayons, or felt pens and paper, are ideal for learners to use to create word sculptures. For example, students can be invited to write a list of words that they think of that relate to a concept they have just studied in class. Then, they are asked to arrange each word on a piece of paper in a pattern of their choosing. Some students may use a spiral pattern for their words, while others use an alphabet letter shape to organize their ideas. There are no limits to form that word sculptures can take. (See Figure 4.4 for a word sculpture that was developed using a computer program)

Figure 4.4 Word Sculpture

In blended or online classes, students create word sculptures electronically in Paint™ or Word™. Alternately, students can use a program such as Word Clouds™ to create word sculptures. Instructors often only need to explain the concept and purpose of a word cloud and digitally savvy students will find a tool to create one.

17. Online Theatre

In online theatre, students do dramatic readings (stories or play) and each student reads a part. This can be done out loud in an Adobe Connect™ session in an online course, or for students who study in person, they can do their readings in front of the classroom. Dramatic readings that relate to course themes can be powerful teaching tools. For example, one instructor in a mental health class engaged students in a story/play about poverty, homelessness, and mental illness. The students did readings from the play that was written by a local author on this theme. Reading the words out-loud enhanced the authenticity of the ideas and experiences and brought the experiences to life. Students report these oral readings are memorable, and because they are so authentic, students find themselves remembering (and reflecting on) the ideas and feelings after the class is over.

In the face-to-face or blended learning environment, students can be formed into groups and given the 'script' for the reading with their parts highlighted. Students take turns reading their parts and then a group leader leads the class in a discussion making connections between characters and experiences in the play and the course materials.

18. Virtual Talking Stick Roundtables

Virtual Talking Stick Roundtables are based upon the practices of some North American Indigenous cultures, who use the sacred practice of the talking stick to give equal voice to all participants (Thunderbird, n.d.). Voice and wisdom are shared using the talking stick. Traditionally, the talking stick starts with one individual who is holding the stick (or other substitute token such as a feather or a stone) speaking his or her thoughts before passing the token to another person. The individual holding the token has the full attention of all present and the opportunity to share his or her thoughts on a topic. This process repeats until all who wish to speak have been given an opportunity to do so. Individuals can choose to pass the token to another, choosing not to speak if they do not have anything they want to contribute.

A talking stick activity can be effective in post clinical debriefing sessions where students can use the passing of the token to ensure everyone has an opportunity to share their ideas and experiences with the others in the class. In other face-to-face scenarios, the talking stick activity can be useful if a delicate or difficult topic (like a conflict situation) needs to be resolved through group discussion.

In online teaching, the Virtual Talking Stick activity starts with the instructor who posts an image of a talking stick (or other token) and an explanation of the traditions behind it in an online forum. The instructor passes a token to another student who then, after speaking, passes it to another student until all students have an opportunity to 'speak.' Students can 'speak' with words, art-forms and images, or poetry. This can be done live in Adobe Connect™, or an online forum with written comments. Students can speak to whatever is on their heart/mind about a question or issue.

This APT can be adapted for use in the face-to-face classroom, by either inviting an Elder from an Indigenous community to come and explain and guide this practice (using a token instead of a talking stick) or through explanation and guidance by the instructor. Students would sit in a circle and give their thoughts and wisdom on a certain topic and then pass the token to another student who would do the same until all students have a chance to speak.

19. Photo Cascades

Based on Photovoice (PV) as a teaching strategy, Photo Cascades encompasses an assortment of photographic images centered around a course theme or concept. The beginning images are presented by the instructor who presents the pictures and poses a reflective question. Next, students are invited to answer the question and to add their own images related to the topic/question. This results in a cascade of images, questions, and responses. The photo cascade activity is typically completed in an online forum. This activity is suitable for all learning environments. (An example of an instructor-led Photo Cascade is presented in Figures 4.5 and 4.6).

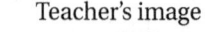

Teacher's image

Figure 4.5 (McLaughlin, 2007)

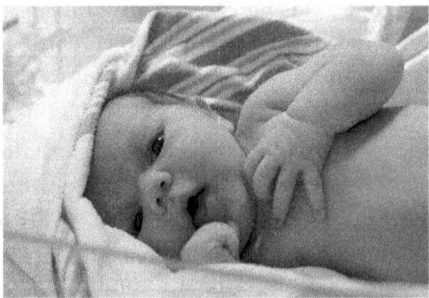

Reflection question --- If you were in charge on immunization programs how would you maximize participation rates?

Student's image

Figure 4.6 (MFer Photography, 2014)

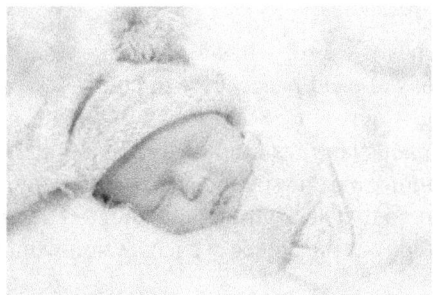

Student's answer – Involve the entire family including fathers in education programs related to the benefits of immunization.

20. My Music Moments

Music is a powerful medium for expression. In this APT students are invited to share self-selected pieces of music that appeal to them and relate their choice to a course concept or theme. For example, lyrics of a music selection may provide students with insights on complex and emotional topics such as end of life, transition, conflict, or aging. Legally downloadable music can be found on websites such as Jamendo where students can search a music database using key words that focus on the concept they are interested in. Students then share their music selection with other class members and provide a written or oral commentary explaining their choice and what they learned from the music. This activity can be used in any learning environment.

21. PD Sculptures

PD sculptures were first used in a second-year nursing course when students were asked to sculpt what burnout looked like to them. To create the PD sculptures, students are given modeling clay or a clay-like material such as Play Dough™ and invited to sculpt a specific concept. Students share their finished sculptures with the class and explain the links between their artwork and the concept.

Face-to-face classroom environments are most conducive to the use of PD sculptures. However, it can be adapted to online classrooms by asking learners to take a photograph of their finished sculpture and then post the image to an online forum with a few sentences describing their sculpture and the conceptual links. Small pots of Playdough ™ can be purchased in volume for a very reasonable price. Alternately, there are recipes online for clay-like materials and students who are studying at a distance can easily make their own sculpting material for this activity.

22. Courtroom Scenes

Courtroom Scenes are an APT that combines drama and learning. Courtroom Scenes are used particularly in courses which focus on legal issues in nursing. Courtroom Scenes start with the instructor finding actual medical/nursing lawsuits from the internet that involve negligence. The instructor outlines one lawsuit for each of a predetermined number of groups of students so that each group has a different lawsuit to work with. Instructors then type out the details of each lawsuit without disclosing the actual outcome.

Students are divided into groups of 5. Each student is given a choice of roles which they can play such as defendant, judge, counsel for the defendant, prosecution, or jury member. Each group is given an envelope which contains specific directions for the activity, the details of the lawsuit, and one three by five-inch card. Students use these cards to record 3 questions each that they will ask the plaintiff or defendant (depending on the role selected).

Students are given twenty minutes for preparation. The instructor prepares name cards with the corresponding names of the courtroom players on them. The classroom is set up with tables/chairs at the front of the class to mimic a courtroom.

The students (in their groups) use all that they have learned about legal issues and negligence to present the 'case' to the rest of the class by acting out the scenario as if in a real courtroom. Students are encouraged to actively 'put on' the various roles as if they were the real characters in the lawsuit.

Props can be used such as a gavel or judge's robe which may be a graduation gown. The cases are presented one by one to the rest of the class. The jury gives a verdict and the judge awards damages. Then the instructor tells them what really transpired in the court case and what damages (if any) were awarded. This activity can be adapted for online and blended learning environments by students acting out their cases in an audio and video-enabled chatroom.

As an alternative to using real lawsuits, disciplinary hearings can be used as the basis of these role plays. Instructors can find details of disciplinary hearings in regulatory publications.

23. Ethics-opoly

Ethics-opoly is a game that is similar to the game of Monopoly™. The game can be played with up to 8 players. The purpose of the game is to help students review concepts that are taught in a nursing class about ethics. Game boards are prepared online with corresponding spaces for street names (such as Allegation Alley or Beneficence Bay) and enlarged and laminated. Two sets of double-sided cards are prepared (using business card templates). On one side of a card, there is an ethics-related question. The second side of a card is labelled 'Ethics Card' or 'Values Cards.' The cards provide the opportunity to test a student's knowledge on ethics-related terms or situations. For example, an Ethics Card might read: Define moral distress. Advance 2 spaces for the correct answer. A Values Card might read: Your personal values conflict with those of your manager. Describe what actions you will take. Advance 3 squares for a correct answer. 'Ethics-Bucks' are also prepared in advance in denominations of $10, $20, $50, $100, and $500. There is one die used for each game.

The goal of the game is to see who can collect the most properties and 'Ethics-Bucks'. Tokens for the game and dice can be purchased at minimal cost. The game is played for 45 minutes. This APT is used for face-to-face classrooms. A digital version could be developed.

24. Obituaries/Music: What do You Want to Be Remembered For?

Students are either provided with the URL to the song, "Say Something" by A Great Big World at https://www.youtube.com/watch?v=-2U0Ivkn2Ds or the instructor plays the YouTube™ video of the song for the class. The instructor relates to the class that everyone may have something to say about their lives, especially at the end of their lives as they come to terms with end-of-life issues. The instructor then gives students the opportunity to write their own obituary assuming that they are 92 years old and have lived a "good" life. Students are reassured that this is a personal activity and that their responses will not be shared with the class. This APT is suitable for all learning environments and promotes reflection and introspection.

25. Morning Coffee Forum

Morning Coffee Forum is an online forum designed to help students and instructors get to know one another. It can be used with individuals or groups and at any point in the semester. There are several variations of the forum. For example, instructors invite students at the beginning of the semester to the Morning Coffee Forum to share something about themselves (such as why they are taking the course or details about their families or pets). The purpose of the activity is to engage in social interaction, identify commonalities, create bonds, and facilitate a sense of community. Instructors engage in the first posting. Students are invited to provide comments on postings.

Another example is the use of the Morning Coffee Forum to bring students together in their groups (after groups are formed for group work or class presentations). Students would meet the people they would be working with in a private forum, to get to know one another, and to discuss important details of the project or presentation.

In another variation, students are invited to come to the Morning Coffee Form and besides introducing themselves, they are invited to post a picture of their favorite coffee cup. The picture, along with a few sentences explaining why this cup is special to them, triggers interaction and often gives memorable details about a particular learner. Students are invited to reply to others' postings and images. Morning Coffee Forum can also be utilized in face-to-face learning environments where students can bring their favorite coffee cup to class in a show-and-tell with classmates.

26. Class Temperature Checks

Class Temperature Checks are used in the middle of a semester to ascertain student feelings and thoughts about a course. Temperature checks are done anonymously to enhance participation. The Class Temperature Checks consist of questions printed on a piece of paper (if done in a face-to-face class) with space for students to write their answers. Students choose to answer - Hot!, Cold or Just Right. Questions could include:

1. I find the pace of the course ---
2. The textbook for the course is ---
3. The amount of group work is ---

Temperature checks give instructors a sense regarding what teaching strategies are working (or not working) and can act as a good feedback mechanism to guide instructors in adjusting teaching approaches or course content. Results of each question are tabulated together, often by administrative assistants. This makes deciphering of the outcomes easy. This APT can be used in any learning environment.

27. Begin with Baroque

Baroque music is not just for lovers of classical music, but can also benefit students in online, blended, or face-to-face classrooms. Composers such as Pachelbel, Vivaldi, Mozart, and Handel have produced classical works of music. Their music, along with the music of other composers from the Baroque Period, has been shown to produce alpha waves which promote relaxation perhaps because this type of music has 60 beats/minute which mimics the normal heartbeat (Blackburn, 2017). Blackburn reports that music has other physiologic effects such as increasing blood flow to the brain, dual brain hemisphere stimulation, enhancing memory retrieval, and greater cerebral cortex activity. Further, Baroque music decreases cortisol levels and decreases both blood pressure and heart rate. Using Begin with Baroque in classrooms before exams or presentations can help students relax and create memory enhancement.

This type of music can also be played when students are doing reflective journaling or studying. Baroque selections can be included in Power Point™ presentations to help the audience to be more attentive and to recall the content shared. A downloadable site that provides freely accessible Baroque period music is "A Baroque Banquet" found at: http://www.baroquecds.com/baroquebanquet.html

28. Gratitude Letters

Gratitude Letters are an APT that is suitable for all learning environments. Instructors invite students to write a Gratitude Letter to other students in the classroom. The students then email the letters to their chosen recipients. Alternately, instructors can write a Gratitude Letter to each student in the class thanking the students for their individual contributions. This can be done in the face-to-face environment with the use of thank you cards. These cards can be distributed near the end of the semester or on the last day of class.

As a variation, students can be encouraged to write Gratitude Letters to their real-life mentors, people who helped shape their attitudes, values, and beliefs. In their letters, students are urged to share details with the mentor of the people they have become, in part because of the mentor's influence. To produce such a Gratitude Letter requires students to engage in self-reflection and analysis. Once the letters are shared with the mentors, relationships may be rekindled and ongoing mentorship is an outcome.

29. Photostories

Photostories involve the use of music, images, and text which are combined in a program such as Movie Maker™. These Photostories can create a great impact on students as they can be evocative in terms of intellect and emotion. Photostories can be used in various ways. For example, Photostories can be used to introduce instructors to their students at the beginning of a semester. Further, Photostories can be used to introduce concepts in a course or to explore meaning. Students are invited to respond to Photostories in an online forum or in written text. Photostories can also be used at the end of the semester for course closure. This APT can be used in all learning environments.

30. Quote Share

Quotations are effective teaching tools. Students can be challenged to find a quote from a famous writer on a specific course topic. For example, in a course on change management, a quick internet search yields hundreds of insightful quotes about problems associated with change. It is easy for learners to find a quote that in a few well-chosen words makes a profound point about a course topic. When these quotes are shared in an online form (or orally in a face-to-face classroom), they often stimulate excellent class discussion and the acquisition of high-order cognitive learning outcomes.

Further, since each learner selects a different quote the nature of the content of the quote can inform the rest of the class about that person. If someone has a great appreciation for humor he or she might select a quote that is funny or quirky. If a student is very serious and scholarly, then the quote selected may reflect this student's nature. In this way, students learn about each other and about course themes through this activity.

31. Elevator Speeches

Elevator Speeches involve creating a speech that can be delivered in the time it takes to get from the ground floor of a building to a few floors above (Cox & Marris, 2011). Cox and Marris describe the necessary components of an effective Elevator Speech as starting with a hook to involve the audience. As the doors close on the elevator the clock starts ticking down and students have three to five minutes to sell themselves, an idea, or a construct. The Elevator Speech ends with concluding statements and concludes when the figurative doors of the elevator open on the desired floor.

This APT can be used in connection to a favorite unit in the course (Cox & Marris, 2011) or with an issue that is relevant to the course. The Elevator Speech is audio-recorded by the student using a device such as a cell phone and is loaded as a MP3 file to an online forum. To make this experience exciting and to create anticipation, the instructor announces to the class several weeks before the Elevator Speeches are due, that there will be an 'Elevator Speeches Awards Ceremony.' Each week prior to the activity this ceremony is mentioned to create student excitement and engagement.

On the day the Elevator Speeches are shared with the class, class members assign a number of 'stars' to each speech, from one to five stars. The instructor tabulates the results. For the awards, categories are created by the instructor, such as Best Elevator Speech, Best Actor, Best Script, Best Sound Effects, etc. It is suggested that the categories stay within a manageable limit for the instructor—enough so that anticipation will be piqued, but not too many to overwhelm the instructor. The instructor then takes all the speeches that were rated five stars and determines what category each Elevator Speech fell into. There will be several nominees in each category. The Elevator Speeches can be adapted for online, face-to-face, or blended classrooms.

In the face-to-face classroom, prior to the day of the Elevator Speech Awards, the instructor will have procured some token of award and a certificate for each 'winner.' The certificates can be easily made using a program such as Word™. For example, Elevator Speeches awards could be small bars of chocolate put into plastic champagne glasses which have been purchased at a local store. Envelopes are prepared prior to the ceremony with the name from each winner of the category in the envelope and the nominees on the outside of the envelope.

The instructor chooses a Master of Ceremonies to narrate the awards ceremony from students in the classroom. Ideally, the Master of Ceremonies is an outgoing student who possesses an element of humor and fun, and who can get the class engaged. The student reads each category and nominees aloud and announces winners. Awards proceed through the various categories until the category of Best Elevator Speech. Anticipation can mount for this final award.

In the online or blended classroom, Elevator Speeches Awards can be given online in various forums prepared by the instructor, or in a forum such as Adobe Connect™. The instructor becomes the Master of Ceremonies for the award ceremony. Students are emailed certificates as their awards.

32. Letter Writing

Letter Writing can be a powerful method of being able to realize growth or verbalize hopes and dreams for the future. Letter Writing, as an APT, can be utilized in several ways. In a first-year clinical, students can be invited to write letters to themselves as the person they will be when they are finished their first clinical. They also write a second letter to themselves as the person they are now as they begin clinical. The students send these letters to their instructor (or alternately give them to their instructor) who then places the two letters from each student in an envelope and returns the envelope to the student at the end of the semester. This allows students to be able to see the growth that they have made over the semester.

Letter Writing can also be used for courses as well. For example, students can write letters in a course on Seniors Health to themselves at present and to their 80-year-old self. As an additional feature, the instructor can give feedback on each letter and put the feedback into the envelope along with the letters.

In the online and blended setting, this APT can be adapted by getting students to send their letters to the instructor in an online forum set up for this purpose. The instructor would provide feedback on the letters and return the letters (along with the feedback) at the end of the semester.

33. Media Collage

Media Collage is an APT where students create either an online collage or a paper collage. This collage can involve watching the news for several weeks and collecting news headlines about a course theme. These headlines are formed into a collage. A Media Collage can also involve using images with text that is relevant to the course or a course topic. In an online or blended course, students can share their Media Collages with other students and the instructor in an online forum, entitled Media Collage, where they post their Media Collage for all students to view. Their collage is accompanied by a paragraph which explains their collage. Students are invited, along with their instructors, to provide feedback on the collage. In the face-to-face learning environment, students can physically create a collage using poster board, glue sticks, and scissors or they can create one electronically.

As a variation, Creative Collage is much like Media Collage but involves a course concept or issue that pertains to the course. Students can use a variety of media to create this collage such as felt pens, crayons, glue sticks and magazine images. Alternately students in a face-to-face classroom can use pen or pencil and a large sheet of paper to create a collage.

34. Narrative Fiction

Narrative Fiction can include television drama, movies, and online videos based on fictional scenarios. These forms of fictional narrative have positive effects on e-learner engagement as they capture learner attention and motivate them to share their views with classmates and with the instructor. Sharing of views is a starting point for discovering commonalities and differences in perspective which stimulates the further exchange of insights in a face-to-face or online classroom.

35. Narrative Weblogs (E-Journaling)

Narrative Weblog can be a learning activity in a course or a way to demonstrate learning. Narrative Weblogs often take the form of e-journaling. Journaling is an important part of learning and assessment of learning. Reflective journals may be especially useful during clinical practicum experiences or as ways to house and share artifacts that allow students to demonstrate learning. These e-portfolios are opportunities for authentic assessment as they allow students to showcase examples that display what they have learned as well as their achievement of meaningful reflection and honest self-awareness.

Journals that are part of e-portfolios can take various forms. Students can add images, audio, video, hyperlinks and other media to their journals. These Weblogs can be kept private and only shared with the instructor or opened more widely to allow classmates to access, and comment, on the blogger's writing. In some courses where a goal is to help learners establish a professional community, a Weblog that is public can be step-in learners connecting with other professionals in their field. Students can easily create a weblog (no advanced computer skills are needed) and in this online space they can post and share ideas, experiences, and insights.

References

Andrews, M., Chapman, B., & Purcell, S. (Directors) (2012). Brave. [Film]. Emeryville, CA: Disney-Pixar Studios.

Austin, W. (2011). Against compassion: Understanding institutional perfidy as evil. *Inter-dsiciplinary.net.* p. 1-11. Retrieved from http://www.inter-disciplinary.net/wp- content/uploads/2011/04/waustinpaper.pdf

Avenet, J. (Director, 1991). Fried Green Tomatoes. [Film]. Hollywood, CA: Universal Pictures.

Blackburn, H. (2017). Music in the classroom. *International Journal of the Whole Child, 2*(1), 26-32.

Cox, A.M., & Marris, L. (2011). Introducing elevator speeches into the curriculum. *Journal of Education for Library and Information Science, 52*(2), 133-141.

De Palma, B. (Director, 1996). Mission impossible. [Film]. Los Angeles, CA: Paramount Pictures.

Janzen, K.J. (2013). Quantum learning environments: Making the virtual seem real in the online classroom. In S. Melrose, C. Park, & B. Perry (Eds.) *Teaching health professionals online: Frameworks and strategies.* Edmonton, AB: AU Press.

Janzen, K.J., & Perry, B. (2014). *The abyss.* Retrieved from http://moments.athabascau.ca/compassion/index.php

Janzen, K.J. (2017). Collective quilting. [Image]. Calgary, Canada

McLaughlin, T. (2007). Brooklyn. [Image]. Creative Commons. Attribution Share alike License 2.0 (Generic 2.0). Changes Made: Color to Black and White. Retrieved from https://www.flickr.com/photos/12738000@N00/406007865/in/photolist-pAsxe9-d878BG-d87a2N-5TdNah-pCtg2w-pCe4d8-pm1aRj-pkZc2g-pAsziQ-6b2r2r-qvNRaw-paezK6-srpLC-EnCd2w-qdUBx-XjN7ro-rYsm4Q-qqS4Ja-qnqVrf-pF1M2E-pxr3op-pPKSeh-iNJkQj-SNess-pm1u6y-AmHzd-pAsp1f-7Pw7KE-d878hC-d879H7-cnK8eN-d878XL-d879id-d878tf-hMLiC4-BSTZB-d879vU-d878PG-ccT4z-4WwpNv-d879SU-bJpfKi-RFZYL9-8yogY3-67mR5M-gFDYQt-6MA8rN-3MArjq-d8798w-29Jm5H

MFer Photography (2014). Attrbution –No Deriv 2.0 Generic (CC by ND-2.0) Retrieved from https://www.flickr.com/photos/fotostalker/14314956573/in/photolist-nNXTS6-Q7q8a-9XcEDy-djJ5L9-7GR5bt-4yCPrM-81khFz-dp2vT-7p8yEu-7p8yKm-68xY9N-5gMBj6-boYFqR-85Y2PS-e7kzuk-WMwEXU-dQ6oSE-mPRqoU-VGZcRa-2en1SX-e2dQD1-edrbBH-GdC68F-WMDu3Y-6stMLU-novtsL-8DPYZm-52bSLP-gCmbZA-5UcZK-ehDTor-5MvWfT-23XyNNf-nTYtmG-7pW1YN-ahyQpa-84PNpS-T5p9co-9kbpPS-aUPUtg-iESmcf-53Edys-6oLgdV-4skPMB-gCng1g-5fjZ3T-gCmKrX-gCmyJM-TrM4tt-a7AuQT

Modsell, S. (2012). Chrysalis. [Image]. Creative Commons Commercial Licence, Changes Made: Color to Black and White Image. Retrieved from https://www.flickr.com/photos/sidm/7026077961/in/photolist-bGSucc-5WenV2-gSTjcf-74NXxH-74SR1o-74STFj-74TNzS-74NXv6-qXqR6y-hwkpwu-QbAod-74NWYv-74TNa9-bvvnPB-74TikW-dpcEat-8vKKtb-4D6uyt-74PcS2-74Txth-4D6uxK-66bisC-74PTXT-bsyje2-7DPzYx-74PhXz-74NZHK-74TbUw-WKdogd-74TDty-WKfBCE-hwmSvz-XKXeYW-rrLs8N-74PBnK-XWN5bA-Y1YBZR-66742r-74PoVn-74T7W9-WKeVyb-4ka3Uq-WKeBYb-zy4gt-bw1qPV-7K6SyT-7vRFWr-4D6uzc-hwkVxQ-74T6Q3

Perry, B. (2006). Using photographic images as an interactive online teaching strategy. *The Internet and Higher Education, 9*(3), 229-240.

Perry, B., & Edwards, M. (2009). Strategies for creating virtual learning communities. In Nursing and Clinical Informatics: Socio- Technical Approaches, B. Staudinger, V. Hob, H. Ostermann, (Eds.). (pp.175-197). Hersey, CA: IGI Global. Retrieved from http://www.igi-global.com

Perry, B., Janzen, K., & Edwards, M. (2011). Creating invitational online learning environments using learning interventions founded in the arts. *eLearning Papers, 27,* 1-4. Retrieved from http//www.elearningpapers.eu

Thunderbird, S. (n.d). *Sacred symbols and their meanings.* Retrieved from http://www.shannonthunderbird.com/Native_contributions.html

Wang, C., & Burris, M. (1997). Photovoice: Concept, methodology, and use for participatory needs assessment. *Health Education Behavior, 24,* 369–387. Retrieved from http://deepblue.lib.umich.edu/bitstream/handle/2027.42/67790/10.1177_109019819702400309.pdf?sequence=2

Chapter 5

The Evidence Base: Past, Present and Future

Research on the use of new educational technologies can lend credibility to the technologies uses. While APTs have been used since 2006, there have been several studies related to APTs which have strengthened conclusions that APTs make credible use of technology. Some make a distinction between high-tech and low-tech teaching strategies. APTs generally fall into the low-tech category as they use simple technology and do not rely on expensive or complex resources. In short, APTs 'work!' This chapter centres on the evidence that demonstrates why and how APTs are effective as teaching strategies. The evidence base in terms of outputs from the research are circumscribed within 26 papers (two in review), six book chapters (one in review), and 33 national and international conference presentations which are all centred on APTs.

The Research Studies: 2006 – 2013

Background

From 2006-2013 APTs have been studied in the course of three funded grants. Beth's first qualitative grant was received in 2006 from the Athabasca University Mission Critical Research Funding for a study of *Graduate Students' Perceptions of the Online Teaching Technologies of Photovoice and Virtual Reflective Centres and their Relationship to Learning Styles*. Beth's second research grant was obtained in 2007 from the Western Region of Canadian Association Schools of Nursing Education Innovation Fund for a study titled, *Interactive Online Teaching Strategies: Using Photographic Images*. The Social Sciences and Human Resources Council of Canada (SSHRC) (national funding agency), granted Beth and Margaret a Standard Research Grant for their study, *An Exploration of How Artistic Pedagogical Technologies Influence Interaction, Social Presence, and Community in the Online Post-Secondary Classroom*. This mixed methods study was carried out between the years 2009 to 2013. Katherine was the research assistant on this SSHRC study between 2010 and 2012.

Thematic Analysis

There are many ways of reporting on the research and outputs. We have chosen to focus on the conclusions and implications of research we conducted between 2006 and 2013 on the effects of APTs in education. Summaries of the outcomes/outputs of the research are outlined in Table 5.1. The results of the outputs were garnered from student qualitative and quantitative surveys.

In order to present these conclusions and implications, we first categorized all outputs in terms of kinds of APTs used and the resulting conclusions and implications. These results were then analyzed using content analysis to ascertain primary themes. Each of the six themes are explicated upon more fully in the next section of this chapter. The themes include: student engagement, meeting of student needs, creativity encouraged, satisfying the quest for 'real,' culture of community, and learning environment.

Student engagement. The theme of engagement encompassed 9/20 outputs in the content analysis (Edwards, Perry, Janzen, & Menzies, 2012; Perry & Edwards, 2009a; Perry & Edwards, 2010a; Perry, Dalton, & Edwards, 2009; Janzen, Perry, & Edwards, 2011a; Janzen, Perry, & Edwards, 2012b; Janzen, Perry, & Edwards, 2012c; Perry, Janzen, & Edwards, 2012; Melrose, Park, & Perry, 2013). Engagement could be described as one of the most sought-after ideals in any classroom. When students are engaged, there is a sense of flow which enlivens students and brings the classroom experience to life. Flow is described by Shernoff, Csikszentmihalyi, Schneider, and Shernoff (2014) as the "culmination of concentration, interest and enjoyment" (p. 475). Flow is considered a basic human psychological need and is linked to wellbeing (Ilies et al., 2017; Van Eck, 2006). Thus flow, or engagement, can and should be highly desired by students and educators alike.

Disengagement of students is such a pivotal issue within post-secondary classrooms today (Chipchase et al., 2017). Alexander's (2015) thesis explored 450 students' levels of disengagement finding that all students in her study possessed a great degree of disengagement. Further, disengagement was found to be part of university culture and a sign that post-secondary education is "deteriorating" (p. 1). This continued deterioration, as noted by Alexander, has been described in the literature since the 1990's (Arum & Roksa, 2011; Chipchase et al., 2017; Cote & Allahar, 2007, 2011; Kuh, 1999; Kuh, Schuh, & White, 1991; Main, 2004;

Washor & Mojkowski, 2014). While we know that engagement is such an important goal for educators, disengagement may be the more important problem to identify and solve.

While engagement has been studied for decades, the study of disengagement (or even a consistent definition of disengagement) is less obvious in the literature (Chipchase et al., 2017). Alexander (2015) describes disengagement stemming from two variables. Physical disengagement which involves students talking to classmates or 'zoning out,' and digital disengagement which is student use of social media devices in class. We expect that as educators you have frequently experienced both types of disengagement. This may leave you wondering, how can this deterioration be halted, reversed, or at the very least contained?

Chipchase and colleagues (2017) suggest that the responsibility for reducing disengagement lies with governments, institutions, and educators themselves. While it would be easier to blame students for disengagement, there is much that can be done to enhance engagement in the nursing classroom. This may leave you wondering, "What can I personally do to promote engagement in my classroom? We propose that APTs can be a part of the solution for learner disengagement.

APTs have the capacity to create flow and engagement, especially in the areas of student attention (Perry, 2006). APTs can provide novel ways of presenting course content that 'perks up' learners as the APTs catch their attention. This can lead to enhanced overall course engagement with content (Perry et al., 2009; Perry & Edwards, 2009; Perry & Edwards, 2010a; Perry et al., 2012a; Janzen et al., 2011a; 2012b). We found that APTs, particularly the use of photovoice, stimulates further discussion which learners often report enhances their engagement.

In digital natives (those born after 1980) engagement could be particularly seen with the use of multiple APTs throughout the semester in face-to-face classrooms (Janzen et al., 2012d). In week one or two, different APTs are introduced in class. For example, in one of our second-year theory classes, we always do a 'mid-term' temperature check' to see how students are feeling about the course. The temperature check has only five anonymous questions. Two of the questions were, "What do you want more of?" and "What do you want less of?" One answer we received from a student was "More coloring!" as she/he expressed how much she/he enjoyed an APT that utilized felt pens and paper. Students can be engaged with the simple and easy. Engagement does not have to involve the latest 'eye popping' high fidelity technology.

Melrose, Park and Perry (2013) also suggest engagement was an outcome of the use of multiple APTs in the online learning environment. This finding was supported by Henrie's (2016) dissertation which focused on the measurement of student engagement in "technology-mediated environments" (p. 1). Both concluded that online environments could provide fertile ground for student engagement especially with the use of APTs (Melrose et al., 2013; Henrie, 2016).

The most studied of the APTs to date is Photovoice. Research on the APT of Photovoice has been done primarily in the online milieu. Engagement has been seen to be one of the most salient outcomes of Photovoice. (For a complete list and description of APTs developed, see Chapter 4).

Meeting of Student Needs. Content analysis revealed 15/20 outputs discussed enhancement of student needs as an outcome of using APTs. These needs met included safety, wellbeing, confidence, trust, risk-taking, intimacy, solitude, and rapport (Edwards et al., 2012d; Perry, 2006; Perry & Edwards, 2009; Perry & Edwards, 2010a; Perry & Edwards, 2010b; Perry et al., 2011a; Perry et al., 2012a; Perry et al., 2011b; Perry et al., 2011c; Perry et al., 2012c; Janzen et al., 2011b; Janzen et al., 2011c; Janzen et al., 2012d;; Janzen, 2013; Melrose et al., 2013). Student needs are discussed in more depth utilizing Maslow's (1954) hierarchy of human needs.

According to Maslow's (1954) hierarchy of needs there are five basic human needs: physiological-survival, safety-security, love-belonging, self-esteem and self-actualization. (see Figure 5.1) Each need must be met in order for the person to rise to the next need level. D'Souza, Adams and Fuss (2015) describe 'D-needs' as being safety, belonging and self-esteem, while 'B-needs' consist in part as self-actualization. We will first discuss D-needs in the context of APTs.

The first level of needs, physiological-survival, is located at the bottom of the needs pyramid. Maslow (1954) proposed that individuals cannot move to another level of the pyramid of needs unless physiological-survival needs are met. We posit that survival can be psychological in nature as well as physiological.

Anecdotally, the second year of nursing education in the face-to-face institution is referred to as the 'suicide semester' by students. The curriculum is very heavy and much is expected for learners. Stress can be so heightened that students can feel like giving up on becoming nurses. Demir, Demir, Bulut and Hisar (2014) denote that stress "is a considerable psychosocial factor that affects students' academic performances and states of wellbeing" (p. 254).

Demir and associates (2014) go on to report that research has demonstrated that student nurses go through more stress than students in other health-related disciplines. Further, nursing students' locus of control can either be internal (students take on a high degree of responsibility) or external (students exhibiting a feeling of loss of control in the learning environment). An external locus of control can lead to students feeling that no matter what they do they cannot succeed as the demands exceed their capabilities (p. 254).

Students with an external locus of control can become 'stuck' in survival mode. In survival mode, the capacity to learn can be considerably decreased. APTs can ameliorate survival mode by making learning 'fun' or allowing for "spontaneous play" (Janzen et al., 2011a, p. 12) A classroom, therefore, can be a place where students can, even for a two-hour block of time, feel a sense that survival mode is not necessary and they can begin to relax. With this relaxation, students can finally learn and feel a sense of trust and safety expressed as increased comfort levels (Perry & Edwards, 2010b; Janzen, 2013).

Safety is the second of five human needs in Maslow's (1954) pyramid. To be secure in the learning environment, safety is of great importance. As James writes, "The ability of individuals needs being met is not only dependent on the individuals themselves; individual environments can have an influence" (2016, p. 9). Our goal as educators is to make the learning environment as safe as possible for students, so they are not just 'surviving' in our classes. What a great loss it would be to have students survive instead of thrive in a classroom. The greatest loss is the attrition of students who have the potential to be successful.

Benson and Dundis (2003) expressed that, as in Maslow's (1954) model, if survival needs are met, then individuals seek safety. Maslow notes that survival "includes freedom from anxiety and stress" (p. 316). Safety extends not only to personal safety but psychological safety within the classroom. While the potential exists for post-secondary classrooms to be places where students feel unsafe, there is also the potential for educators to create learning environments that are full of wonder. One way educators can create these ideal places for learning includes the careful crafting of learning experiences such as APTs.

Our research has shown that APTs can support a sense of safety and comfort in online classrooms (Perry & Edwards, 2009a; 2009b; 2010b; Melrose et al., 2013). We have also found that APTs can also facilitate a sense of safety in face-to-face classrooms (Janzen et al., 2012c). In both online and face-to-face learning environments, students can feel free to express their opinions and values through APTs without fear of censure as there are no right or wrong answers in APT activities (Perry & Edwards, 2010a). Further, most times the APTs are not counted as a part of the summative learner evaluation, so there are essentially "no marks" for participating in APTs. APTs are usually offered as optional activities and learners are invited to participate.

One particular APT was a letter writing exercise where third-year nursing students who were taking Seniors Health, were asked to write a letter from their 'now' self to their 80-year-old self. In this letter, they were asked to share their fears, hopes, and dreams as a senior. They were then asked to write a letter from their 80-year-old self to their now self to share the wisdom and advice that their 80-year-old self had to give them. This activity was not graded, yet every student in the class participated and shared their letters with me. We were so touched with the honesty in the writing, particularly the sense of safety and trust they must have felt to share their deep feelings with their instructor. The letters truly humbled me as we read them and provided feedback to each student. The fears they expressed were very genuine, and their hopes and dreams made our souls touch the sky for them as human beings. We knew from what they shared in these letters that nursing will be in good hands when we became seniors. We were honored to be their instructors. If there had not been a sense of safety and trust, the contents of the letters could have been quite different. Students would have guarded what they wrote. APTs have the potential in safe environments to bring out the best in students. Thus, APTs can positively influence rapport and trust between learners and instructors (Janzen et al., 2011a).

The third level of Maslow's (1954) hierarchy of needs is the need of belonging. When we look back to our days of being in nursing school and living in residence, we realize that it was the sense of belongingness that made a positive difference. Our nursing colleagues continue to have nursing reunions 30 and 40 years after they have graduated. This speaks to the collegiality of nursing education. Nurses share a special bond with each other as nursing students do. Friends in nursing school can become friends for life.

Social needs of belonging can be heightened through the use of APTs (Perry & Edwards, 2012b). A further outcome of APTs is intimacy (Janzen et al., 2011a; Melrose et al., 2013). APTs help create a sense of community through shared experiences which are literally 'shared-with' one another other. This can result in social connectedness (Perry et al., 2009b). A knowing of self and others, a shared sense of purpose and values, and meaningful interactions in enhanced student-to-student learning also have been observed with the use of APTs (Perry & Edwards, 2009a; 2009b).

For example, while in the clinical realm (especially in first-year student clinical groups) students and instructors can bond. We believe that almost every nurse or nursing student can recall their very first nursing experience in the hospital, complete with their instructor's name and a recollection of how they felt and how their day went. Instructors are such an important part of this very first day. Such is the power of community.

We all have had experiences being the clinical coordinator for first-year students. After the students' first clinical day in the hospital, We post an APT of Photovoice showing an image of a mother duck trying to get her little ducklings to follow her up a set of stairs in an urban center. The mother duck is on the top stair. One little duckling is struggling to get up the first stair. The caption we put on this image is: "Some days are harder than others. Today you took your first giant step into the world of nursing." It has been gratifying to have students email us about the personal impact of this Photovoice. We know that APTs can make a positive difference for learners.

APTs can also help a clinical or academic group achieve closure (Perry & Edwards, 2010b). For example, we share a piece of poetry, entitled, "Nursing is More" (Perry, 2009) at the concluding post-conference for first-year nursing students. Then we express our feelings about the poem and invite students to express theirs. Together we reminisce about our experiences during clinical, what nursing means to each person, and what we are going to take away from this clinical time together. This APT not only provides a springboard for further discussion, it can allow students to gain a sense of closure (Perry & Edwards, 2010b).

APTs can foster wellbeing and confidence—both desirable psychological states (Janzen et al., 2012a, Perry, 2006). If wellbeing and confidence are fostered in students, the result is students who believe they can succeed. In turn, students who experience a sense of wellbeing may become more self-aware and feel at ease in the classroom (Janzen et al., 2012a). We have found that university students attend classes because they genuinely want to be there. Students want to learn and to do well academically. They have aspirations, dreams, hopes, and goals that depend in part on their educational achievements. At times all that is needed for them to achieve these is self-confidence.

For example, think of student nurses doing their 'first.' Their first dressing change, their first tracheostomy care, their first care for a newborn. Students may feel nervous at the beginning, but confidence grows with practice. This is similar to participation in APTs. Students, when introduced to APTs for the first time, may be a bit anxious about doing an APT but more often we find that they are intrigued and excited as APTs allow self-expression (Perry et al., 2012c). Solitude and self-introspection are also important outcomes for students who engage in APTs as certain APTs focus on what is going on inside of students' minds and on their experiences and can consequently result in sense-making (Janzen et al., 2011a).

If used throughout the semester, students begin to look forward to the next APT and participate with increasing confidence (Janzen et al., 2012a). Increased confidence is an outcome of the use of APTs (Janzen et al., 2012c), especially when students feel valuable as individuals (Simons, Irwin & Drinnien, 1987). Further, as "individuals progresses [through a semester using APTs] their confidence level grows and there is greater opportunity to obtain rewards, recognition and positive appraisals" (Benson & Dundas, 2003, p. 317; Janzen, 2013). APTs can foster the rewards of recognition and positive appraisal from other students and from instructors. Students can find and share their personal voice through APTs (Janzen et al., 2012a)

Wellbeing is so very important in today's classrooms. Students face multiple threats to their wellbeing outside the classroom—simply in part by living in a tumultuous world. With images and videos of terrorism and war viewed on demand through media devices, students need an alternative space where wellbeing can flourish. APTs can provide such a place and invite inspiration (Janzen et al., 2012a).

For example, nurse educator and psychologist Sharon Moore uses a form of APTs where she posts a photographic image and a quotation before every unit of a course (Melrose et al., 2013). This allows for student reflection. The images that Moore posts are stunning, and students find it inspirational when they come to know that their instructor took these images herself. This "wow" factor continues throughout the semester with each successive image and quotation posted. This APT can inspire wellbeing in students and give students a chance to get to know their instructor (the photograph) on a more personal level.

When viewed through Maslow's (1954) hierarchy of needs, wellbeing and confidence can be likened to the fourth and the final fifth (highest) level of the Maslow's model. Self-esteem needs become an expression of increasing confidence (Benson & Dundis, 2003). Benson and Dundis (2003) express this presenting an opportunity to "feel and actually be more productive in . . . the [learning or] work environment" (p. 317). It has been said that confidence breeds confidence, and confidence can move students into the realm of self-actualization once self-esteem needs have been satisfied. Education benefits from "person growing" approaches which APTs promote (Simons et al., 1987, p. 2). Respect, appreciation, and validation are examples of self-esteem needs (D'Souza et al., 2015) which APTs promote in terms of positive affirmations (Edwards et al., 2012) This has been seen with the use of APTs in terms of encouraging social engagement with other students and instructors (Perry et al., 2012c).

We propose that self-actualization can be expressed as wellbeing. Self-actualization is considered to be a measure of fulfillment or the realization of human potential (Block, 2011; James, 2016; McLeod, 2007/2013). While wellbeing has been previously defined very narrowly, there is a call to explicate wellbeing in terms of holism and to embrace definitions that define wellbeing in terms of relationships and "enhancing educational experiences" (Soutter, O'Steen & Gilmore, 2014, p. 497). Michalos (2007) takes a more robust view of education, and states that "education can have an 'enormous influence on happiness'" (p. 2) or wellbeing. APTs can be seen to promote both relationships and enhanced educational experiences (Perry & Edwards, 2009b; Perry et al., 2011c).

Wellbeing in the context of APTs is an outcome of participating in APT activities (Janzen et al., 2012a). APTs promote risk-taking (Perry et al., 2011c; Perry et al., 201b) which is another outcome of self-actualization (Benson & Dundis, 2003). This culminates in developing one's own potential and to reaching toward new learning (Benson & Dundis, 2003) which can effectively promote growth as a student and as a human being (Perry et al., 2012b). APTs can foster the capacity for inspiration and influence (Janzen et al., 2012c) both wonderful qualities for a nurse to possess in order to be prepared to influence the profession of nursing. Finally, APTs can empower students to enact change—in themselves, their classrooms, their workplaces, and their world (Janzen et al., 2012b). This outcome is relevant to the research we have done that concluded that APTs create cultures of community in learning environments.

Creating a Culture of Community. Creating a culture of community is one of the most pervasive outcomes of research related to APTs. Just in sheer numbers, creating a culture of community has been focused on as an outcome of APTs in 18/20 outputs (Edwards et al., 2012; Perry, 2006; Perry & Edwards, 2009a; 2009b; 2010a; 2010b; Perry et al., 2011b; Perry et al., 2012; Perry et al., 2012a; 2012b; Janzen et al., 2011a; 2011b; Janzen et al., 2012a; 2012b; 2012c; 2012d; Janzen, 2013; Melrose et al., 2013). The outcome of creating cultures of community is discussed in the following section.

Going back to Maslow's human needs, Maslow in 1964 and 1968 added self-transcendence as a sixth human need. Transcendence is understood as a situation, or situations, where a person is able to "obtain a unitive consciousness with other humans" (Venter, 2016, p. 3). Venter explained this in terms of people not being solely defined by their environments. Venter explained, "Without distortion of their own cultural identity or developing crippling insecurity, they can identify and side with other people, different groups, entities, and causes, and nationalities" (p. 4). Maslow's self-transcendence relates to the outcome of creating cultures of community. (See Figure 5.2)

D'Souza and colleagues (2015) discuss self-transcendence as "a need to further a cause beyond the self and to experience communion beyond the boundaries of the self through peak experiences" (p. 29). In a community, the self (although still present and having a need for self-actualization) is secondary to the experience of the communal in the online and face-to-face learning environment. Although it is easier to create a community in the face-to-face environment through physical presence and physical activities as groups, APTs can enhance the creation of community in the online learning milieu (Perry & Edwards, 2009b). This is expressed as creating a culture of community (Perry & Edwards, 2009a).

If D'Souza and colleagues (2015) definition of self-transcendence is accepted, then the seeking of a cause beyond self, and the experience of communion beyond the boundaries of self, become wrapped up in developing a new culture which is beyond one's own. "A culture of community is defined as shared culture in the online [and face-to-face] classroom including shared values, norms and beliefs" (Perry & Edwards, 2010a, p. 132). This culture becomes that of the learning community.

The learning community has a unique culture all of its own, just as each individual university has its own culture. There are many variables which contribute to an educational culture. Gorski and Swalwell (2015) name these as: competence, expertise, applicable teaching, accountable teaching, multicultural education, inter-cultural education, and cross-cultural education (p. 222). Gorksi (2016) adds literacy equity to these variables. These variables could be understood as the values upon which educational institutions stand. We submit that each classroom develops a culture of its own. This is usually accomplished with intention from the instructor in developing presence (social, cognitive, and teaching) (Garrison, 2016) and strategic learning strategies and activities. We also propose that students play a large part in developing classroom culture in terms of student needs, capabilities, and interests, among other attributes.

A culture of community can develop on its own over the course of a semester, but intentionality (Perry & Edwards, 2009b) and an invitational instructor stance (Janzen, 2012a; Melrose et al., 2013; Perry et al., 2012) can strengthen the culture of community. A culture of community transcends, and yet welcomes, each individual's own sense of culture. This paradox allows engagement and commitment on a continuum of a classroom's culture of community.

> *Maslow reasoned that a person that transcends their culture is not alienated from it—they are not separated from it. But they are not grounded or anchored in their own culture alone.*
> Henry J. Venter, 2016

In the online learning environment, some students feel that they are in "a classroom of one" (Janzen et al., 2012a, p. 28). Relegated to sitting in front of a computer screen can feel isolating, and at times lonely, as online learners persist in their studies. In the same vein, in face-to-face learning environments, students can feel like they are invisible and that even their names are not known to instructors. In essence, learners can feel like they are just another cog in the wheel (Janzen, 2013). APTs can help learners develop feelings of social connectedness (Perry et al., 2009). APTs ameliorate the sense of being alone by encouraging a shared sense of values and purpose among class participants (Perry & Edwards, 2009a). APTs also help by enhancing student-student learning (Perry & Edwards, 2011b). When students learn from each other, this learning engenders respect and furthers trust among peers (Perry & Edwards, 2009b; Perry et al., 2011c; Melrose et al., 2013). This results in a knowing of self, and others, and in interactions that are meaningful (Perry et al., 2009a). Thus APTs can facilitate interpersonal and intrapersonal social presence (Perry & Edwards, 2010a).

One APT activity which involves trust, respect, and interpersonal/intrapersonal social presence (and creates a sense of community) is titled "Courtroom Scenes" (Janzen et al., 2017). In second year nursing theory, a required course component is the topic of legal issues in nursing. At the end of the lecture, students engage in Courtroom Scenes where students enact a real nursing court case or regulatory body disciplinary case. The classroom is divided into 8 groups, each with a group being given their own Courtroom Scene or Disciplinary Case. Students are called upon to use all they have learned to construct their assigned court or disciplinary case. Each student takes a role such as a judge, prosecutor, defendant, jury member and so on. The classroom comes alive as the court case is presented, arguments engaged in, decisions of guilt/innocence made, and damages awarded.

There have been some amazing mock courtroom scenes presented over the years. Students really 'get into' the roles that they take on. A toy gavel, which makes various noises when used, adds humor to the experience. The damages students award are usually much less than one would see in a real courtroom decision. At the end of each Courtroom Scene, the students find out "the rest of the story" (Watson, 2014, para. 4) and the real decisions that came from their specific courtroom case is revealed by the instructor.

The Encouragement of Creativity. We have found that APTs stimulate, as well as encourage, creativity. References to creativity were found in 9/20 outputs (Perry, 2006; Edwards et al., 2012a; Perry & Edwards, 2009b, 2010a; Perry et al., 2011, 2012a; Janzen et al., 2011a; 2011b; 2012a). As creativity was previously discussed in Chapter 3 in depth, this section of the chapter will focus on research findings and examples of specific activities related to creativity encouragement.

Photovoice, the use of a photographic image and a reflective question, captures "student attention, and stimulates creative thinking" (Perry, 2006, p. 229). The students' ability to make links between photographic images and abstract concepts is enhanced (Perry, 2006; Perry & Edwards, 2009b). When students are able to make these links through the creative arts, we propose that learning is enhanced. This learning is not only seen academically but creatively, as students further their imaginative skills (Perry et al., 2012c). Optimal learning is embraced through the various multi-dimensions explored when students take a creative stance in the learning activities (Janzen, 2013).

Encouragement of creativity is also seen in the learning activities such as Conceptual Quilting and Collective Quilting which have been utilized in both online and face-to-face learning environments. In the quilting exercises, students are invited to make quilts of some descriptions (some are virtual in online environments, others are made of paper quilt squares in face-to-face learning). Each quilt square represents a concept, idea, or a learning that the student identifies be remembered (and used) after the course is completed. Both types of quilting are used as capstone activities. As noted, in the online learning environment the quilt is constructed electronically, while in the face-to-face learning environment the quilt is constructed from actual quilt squares with lined paper stapled to them for students to write on. In both cases, the quilts, once constructed, are presented to the class either as a real tangible collection of quilt squares in a face-to-face class or in an electronic quilt gallery in online learning. This public display of individual quilts helps stimulate further discussion, solidifies course concepts by providing a review of a broad spectrum of course concepts, and assists with closure for class members (Perry, 2009b; Perry & Edwards, 2010a; 2010b). The quilting also helps increase engagement with course content because the creative is engaged (Perry et al., 2012a).

Play is also encouraged—individually and collectively (Janzen, 2013). This can be seen through the different art mediums which we have chosen to use in the classroom. While some mediums are purely electronic in nature in the online classroom, other mediums are more tangible and include Playdough™, felt pens and paper, music, drama, and magazines for Creative Collage. Play is also strongly linked to the creative.

For example, the spoken word was used creatively by a student group who was doing a class presentation. One of the students in the group introduced the presentation by performing a rap song composed by the student for the presentation. The rap tune immediately caught the attention of all students. Laughter and delight were both outcomes of this student's work as his peers all clapped and whistled after he finished his song. The inclusion of a creative rap with lyrics relevant to the presentation topic set a very positive tone for the rest of the presentation which employed several other creative arts-based strategies.

If the instructor uses APTs in the classroom, then it is as if the instructor gives permission for students to also use APTs in their written and oral assignments. We have found that the more creative we are in the classroom, the more creative students are in return. This results in stunning presentations and written work. Students are invited to use their imaginations and their imaginations can take them anywhere.

One example of this is an APT that encourages creativity is called an Elevator Speech. Elevator Speeches a learning activities were described as early as 2011 by Cox and Marris. These authors defined an elevator speech as, "a statement of who you are and what you can offer, brief enough to make a point in the time you might travel with someone a few floors in an elevator" (p. 332). APT Elevator Speeches can be utilized in online, blended, or face-to-face learning environments. In a capstone theory course on leadership, fourth-year nursing students are invited to make an audio elevator speech about an issue in nursing today.

One student who was extremely creative not only prepared an Elevator Speech but created it with the sounds of an elevator (including elevator music) and two distinct people speaking (the Prime Minister of Canada and herself). She changed her voice when presenting her Elevator Speech to represent each of the participants. It was very realistic, creative, and was a joy to listen to as she very effectively made her arguments on her chosen issue in an original way.

Satisfying the Quest for Real. In the online learning environment, the quest for real can be both difficult and ongoing. While it may appear to learners that nothing is real in an asynchronous, online course while interacting on a computer screen, APTs can make these courses come alive. It is noted that the concept of real is mentioned in 11/20 outputs (Perry, 2006; Perry & Edwards 2010a; 2010b; Perry et al., 2012a; 2012b; 2012c; Janzen et al., 2011a, 2011b, 2012b; Janzen, 2013; Melrose et al., 2013).

We devoted a whole paper as an output of the third research grant (SSHRC) on how Photovoice assisted students and instructors to become real to each other in the online environment (Janzen et al., 2011a). The concept of real has come through many times in other literature we have written. Simply put, online environments can become very 'real' to all participants when APTs are used as learning activities.

This real can extend to face-to-face and blended learning environments as well. With large class sizes, the ability to really get to know one's instructor can be minimal. This can be seen in terms of the use of teaching assistants or the time schedule of the instructor being limited for one to one consultation. How does an instructor become real to his/her students and how do students become real to their instructor? Again we suggest that APTs can be part of the solution.

In online classes, Beth creates a video podcast of herself in her home office to introduce herself to her students. Katherine uses a digital photo story to introduce herself and becomes real to her students. These two APT strategies allow for a very personal touch to the introductions of an instructor to a class. In addition, we use storytelling throughout the semester to engage students, promote interest, and to link course concepts to one another and to relevant theory.

For example, we believe that stories have great power to influence and change lives. In our second-year theory classes, many stories are told. In student evaluations of the course and instructor, this is one of the student's favorite parts of the class. The stories make us real to the students as the stories express emotion, captivate, and pique interest as class concepts become alive. Our stories reveal carefully selected details of our personal values and experiences (those that are relevant for the learners) and this helps them get to know us as their instructor, in an authentic and meaningful way.

One story we tell second-year theory students in a unit on death and dying is the story of Mrs. 'J.' Mrs. 'J' was admitted to the surgery ward of a large urban hospital. She had gastrointestinal issues for almost a year. All the tests that they had done on her came back negative. Mrs. 'J' pleaded with her physician to do exploratory surgery to determine the problem. She related if they could find nothing wrong then she would just 'live with it.'

When the attending surgeon did a laparotomy, he found end-stage small bowel carcinoma. He placed a catheter into her bowel to drain stomach contents and sutured her up. She had an epidural for pain control. One day Katherine was in her room visiting with her and she got very quiet. She asked her, "Am I going to die?" She said none of the family members would talk about it to her and that she was desperate for an answer to this question.

Being a nurse, it was known that she wouldn't recover. Katherine gently took her by the hand and said, "Yes, you are going to die." You see, she was Katherine's mother-in-law. She sighed a great sigh of relief and told Katherine that she had suspected this and was glad to know. She told Katherine that this would give her some time to get her affairs in order. She died two weeks later.

We tell this personal story students to introduce death and dying and a discussion of the ethics of telling individuals they are dying. Through the story, the students see that Katherine is a real person—not just an instructor (Perry & Edwards, 2009). The sharing of real stories can open students and the classroom to further, fuller, and deeper discussion. Sharing of stories also helps students and instructors create a sense of intimacy among themselves (Melrose et al., 2013). Human presence can also be demonstrated through stories (Perry, 2006) as well as a sense of humanness (Perry et al., 2011c). This can result in more authentic interactions (Perry et al., 2010b).

The student's become more real to us as instructors through the APTs they engage in. Previously, we have used the examples of two letter-writing exercises. Students became real in terms of sharing their deepest thoughts and fears; their hopes and dreams in the letters shared with instructors.

Katherine has a bulletin board in her office at the university where she displays students' work (with their permission). She also has an 'open door' policy where students can drop by at any time they wish. As long as her office door is open, they know they are welcome. Sometimes they come just to chat, other times with specific concerns. Students have asked if she would put their APT work on display on her bulletin board. They have expressed feelings of pride and accomplishment when they see their work displayed when they come and visit her office.

In the online learning environment, Conceptual Quilting helps instructors also see their students as being 'real' (Perry & Edwards, 2010a). Each quilt that is created tells a story of that student. As instructors view the quilts and have a quilt display for the whole class to view, students and instructors can get to know each other better.

In the APT of Collective Quilting in the face-to-face classroom, each student creates as single quilt square writing on it what they are going to take away from the class (Janzen et al., 2012d). Learners then come to the front of the room and read their square to the class. Following this, the students lay their squares down on the floor making a quilt. When students talk about their square, they share an understanding of what was most important to them in the course. In addition, the instructor can come to know what concepts were most salient for students. Other specific APTs are often mentioned in the quilt squares as being the most important experience of the course for students because these gave them the opportunity to express themselves as real individuals. Collectively APTs can "provide an acceptable avenue for self-disclosure" (Perry et al., 2011c, p. 3).

The Learning Environment. The theme, the learning environment, seems to encapsulate all other themes. In terms of outputs, this theme was one of the most prolific. Different aspects of the learning environment are outlined in 17/20 outputs (Edwards et al., 2012; Perry, 2006; Perry & Edwards, 2009; Perry & Edwards, 2010a, 2010b; Perry et al., 2012; Perry et al., 2012a; Perry et al., 2012c; Janzen et al., 2011a, 2011b, 2012a; Janzen et al., 2012b, 2012c, 2012d; Janzen, 2013; Melrose et al., 2013).

The learning environment in which APTs have been used is best described as 'invitational' (Janzen et al., 2012a; Perry et al., 2011c, 2012a, 2012b; Melrose et al., 2013). This is perhaps one of the most distinctive attributes of utilizing APTs in the learning environment. In short, APTs can "enhance learning environments" in very tangible ways (Perry et al., 2011c, p. 3; Perry & Edwards 2010a). Students are invited by their instructors to engage in learning fully in all quantum dimensions, especially in the social (Perry et al., 2009a; 2009b; Perry & Edwards, 2010a, 2010b, 2012c), spiritual and cultural (Janzen et al., 2011b), technological (Janzen et al., 2012c, 2012d); affective (Janzen, 2013, Melrose et al., 2013) and cognitive (Perry & Edwards, 2010b). In addition, APTs have links to behavioral, experiential, and corporeality dimensions (Janzen et al., 2012d).

A single APT can touch upon several quantum dimensions at the same time. For example, in the fourth year theory course, Trends and Issues in Leadership, we use poetry to gather several quantum dimensions into one activity. The cluster of concepts we visit in that class includes compassion fatigue, compassion, and burnout as these are very salient issues for the students' final class in the curriculum. At the end of our presentation, we recite a poem by E.E. Cummings (1954/1994) a famous American poet. The ". . . wind has blown the rain away and blown the sky away and all the leaves away, and the trees stand. . . [and] the trees [still] stand" (stanza 1, 4).

We relate this to the strength that nursing students have. The rain and sky and leaves on the trees may blow away, but nurses can still stand. We let the students know that they can still stand amid the pressures and issues that they will face (and are facing) in nursing/nursing school. In addition, We relate that the group of students that we teach are strong and capable enough to handle the winds that will regularly come to them. We express our belief in them. Invariably, the students feel a multitude of emotions from the recital of this poem. This APT calls upon the quantum dimensions of affective (emotion), cognition (thinking about what the poem means), and experiential (comparing it to their own experiences with compassion fatigue and burnout). Human interactivity is stimulated by the sharing of this poem (Perry, 2006). Following is another example of how an APT used in a second theory course invites learners to utilize multiple learning dimensions.

Specifically, in the course Theoretical Foundations, students in groups are called upon to do group presentations on a concept of their choice. As the instructor, we begin by modelling how this is to be done by presenting our own concept(s). We have chosen compassion, compassion fatigue, and burnout as the concepts that we present. We have chosen to utilize the APT of parallel poetry as a way to encourage students to really think about what they have taken away from our presentation. Also, the parallel poetry guides them to think about how compassion fatigue effects them. We first present them with a poem—either one that we write or a poem from another author-and then they write their own poem in response to the poem we offer. APTs stimulate creative thinking and the outputs from various activities can demonstrate this (Perry, 2006).

One instructor poem we have used is the following. It was written by Jack (2017) who conducted a study of "The Meaning of Compassion Fatigue to Student Nurses" (p. 5). The poem is called *Professional Widow*. We share part of it here:

> It broke my heart to watch you suffer
> "Chin up chick, you must get tougher"
> Came the cries of camaraderie
> "Concentrate now, that's an artery!"
> I sought advice and found the strength
> To keep my feelings at arm's length
> Respect your boundaries, just pretend
> Be your protector, not your friend

This next poem is an example of an untitled parallel poem which was written by a student in response to the instructor's poem above.

> Who am I to complain?
> No license, no title, no right.
> Who am I to feel stressed?
> Less patients, less workload, less responsibility.
> Who am I to feel hopeless?
> No days off, No pay, No way.
> Who am I to complain?
> Less experience, less respect, less confidence.
> Who am I to wanna change?
> I'm just from a lower league.
> Who am compassion fatigue.

(Personal communication, J. Ekstroem,
July 15, 2015, used with permission)

We believe that instructors desire interactions in their classrooms and rate this among one of the indicators of a successful classroom experience. There is almost nothing worse as an instructor than asking a question in class and having no one reply even after 10 or 15 seconds of silence. I think we have all had this experience. APTs can offer a way to fill awkward silence with learning by encouraging interaction.

Specifically, APTs encourage interactivity (Perry & Edwards, 2009b) and initiate, sustain, and enhance interactions among students, as well as between instructors and students (Perry et al., 2012a; Janzen, 2013; Janzen et al., 2012d). Perry, Edwards and Menzies (2012) found APTs trigger, sustain, and enhance interaction in online courses. In short, APTs invite participation (Janzen et al., 2012a).

Table 5.1 The Outputs: 2006-2013

Year	Output/Type of Publication	Author(s)	APTs Utilized	Conclusions/Implications
2006	Using photographic images as an interactive online teaching strategy (paper)	Perry	Photovoice	-"Captured students' attention, stimulated creative thinking, and created community" (p. 229) -Student engagement and focus of student attention -Enhanced ability to make links between photographic image and abstract concepts -Manifested human presence ('real') -Stimulated human interactivity
2009	Photographic images as an interactive online teaching technology: Creating online communities (paper)	Perry, Dalton & Edwards	Photovoice	-Course engagement -Learning environment enhancement -Development of "social connectedness" (p. 106)
2009	Creating a culture of community in online courses (paper)	Perry & Edwards	Photovoice, Conceptual Quilting & Online Point-counter-point debates	-Shared sense of values and purpose -Knowing of self and others -Meaningful interaction -Increased sense of instructor being 'real' -Culture of community -Informs course design -Facilitates the "the experience of shared classroom community" (p. 1)
2009	Strategies for creating virtual learning communities (book chapter)	Perry & Edwards	Photovoice, Virtual Reflective Centers, Conceptual Quilting, The Great Debate, Point-Counter-point Reflection	-Captures attention -Stimulates creativity -Creates community -Promotes engagement -Encourages abstract thinking -Helps students take risks -Assists educators to convey a sense of self in community -Encourages interactivity -Enhances learner-learner learning -Fosters intimacy -Supports safe learning environment -Establishes meaningful connections, -Develops relationships

				-Stimulates self-interaction and reflection -"Bring[s] effective closure to an online course" (p. 190)
2010	Creating a culture of community in the online classroom using artistic pedagogical technologies (book chapter)	Perry & Edwards	Virtual Reflective Centers, Conceptual Quilting. Photovoice	-Shared sense of values and purpose -Knowing of self and others -Creates meaningful interaction -Increases sense of instructor/students being 'real' -Develops a culture of community -Facilitates interpersonal and intrapersonal social presence -"Allows participants to systematically reveal more of their personal values, beliefs and priorities" (p. 138) -Promotes involvement -Provides tangible evidence of attendance -Encourages engagement -Fuels motivation -Facilitates cycle of meaningful interaction, authentic ongoing social presence and community culture -Engagement in higher order thinking
2010	Interactive teaching technologies that facilitate the development of online learning communities in nursing and health studies (paper)	Perry & Edwards	Photovoice, Conceptual Quilting, & Virtual Reflective Centers (role playing simulation exercises)	-Social linking with other students -Cognitive stimulation -"Sense of an immediate presence of the instructor" (p. 157) -Provided broad spectrum review of course -Reflection on learning -Assess impact of students/instructor on individual -Enhanced course closure -"Positive influence on spirit of the class" (p. 158) -Structured activity that allowed interpersonal safety; social bonding
2011	Becoming real: Using the artistic pedagogical technology of Photovoice as a medium to becoming real to one another in the online	Janzen, Perry & Edwards	Photovoice	-Presence of authentic voice in students -Encourages engagement -Sustains authentic interactions -Allows for "spontaneous play" (p. 12) -Creation of intimacy -Fosters meaning-making -Satisfies the criteria for an authentic medium

	environment (paper)			-Development of trust
2011	Aligning quantum learning with instructional design: Exploring the seven definitive questions (paper)	Janzen, Perry & Edwards	Photovoice, QL	-Facilitates holistic learning, arts-based learning and holistic development -Assists "students to move beyond dimensions of technology and virtuality (become 'real')" (p. 7) in the online classroom -Fosters spiritual and cultural cues
2011	Creating invitational online learning environments using arts-based learning (paper)	Perry, Janzen & Edwards	Reflective Poetry, Minute at the Movies Analyses, 'Our Community' Soap Scenes, Theme Songs	-"APTs provide an acceptable avenue for self-disclosure" (p. 3) -Enhances familiarity -Allows risk-taking -Heightens trust and respect -Encourages diversity and creativity -Promotes group optimism -APTs "enhance learning environments" (p. 3)
2012	A classroom of one is a community of learners: Paradox, artistic pedagogical technologies, and the invitational online classroom (paper)	Janzen, Perry & Edwards	Photovoice	-Students are able to experience freedom and constraint -Promotes engagement and stimulates further discussion -Openness encourages authentic responses -Students accept each other as human -Honors stories of students and discipline -Instructor's presence very meaningful -Provides solitude in terms of time and space -Personal voice found in students -Draws upon student artistic ability -Fosters wellbeing and confidence
2012	Using invitational theory to understand the effectiveness of artistic pedagogical technologies in creating an "invitational classroom" in the online educational milieu (paper)	Perry, Edwards, Menzies, Janzen	Photovoice, Parallel Poetry, Conceptual Quilting	-Amplifies quality of interactions -Heightens sense of community -Furthers the application of course content

2012	Creating an "invitational classroom" in the online educational milieu (paper)	Perry, Janzen & Edwards	Parallel poetry, Conceptual Quilting & Photovoice	-Initiates, sustains and enhances interactions between and among students as well as instructors and students -Contributes to positive tone in classes -Fosters sense of humanness -Invitation to take risks -Develops authentic interactions -Engagement with course content -Increases sense of community
2012	Using the artistic pedagogical technology to promote interaction in the online post-secondary classroom: The student's perspective (paper)	Edwards, Perry, Janzen & Menzies	Photovoice, Mentions drama in the form of online role playing, Movie Analysis, Music in the form of theme song, Literary in form of Story-telling, story-writing and Parallel Poetry	-"Positive influence on course interactions" (p. 32) -Increased sense of community -Enhanced comfort in online milieu -Increased knowing of self, other students and instructor -Positive affirmation from others (Student/Instructor) -Presence of "nurturing connections" (p. 40) -Promoted creativity, instilled energy, allowed emotion, and evident enthusiasm - "Positive growth and development" (p. 40) -Allowed transformative environment
2012	Using the artistic pedagogical technology of photovoice to stimulate interaction in the online post-secondary classroom: The teachers' perspective (paper)	Perry, Edwards & Menzies	Photovoice	-Triggers interaction -Sustains interaction -Enhances interaction -Diverse perspectives were welcomed -All opinions honored and valued -Invitational environment -Significant relationship building (student-student/instructor-student) -Instructors become "tangible" (p. 126)
2012	The entangled web: Quantum learning, quantum learning environments and Web technology (paper)	Janzen, Perry & Edwards	Photovoice, Mention made of parallel poetry, Conceptual Quilting, Word Sculptures, Online Theatre, Conceptual	-APTs epitomize quantum learning environments (QLEs) -Provides links to the temporal and virtual -Invites participation -Infinite potential exists for creativity, developing constructs, ideas and meaning -Fosters community as well as individual learning -Contributes to students' ability for thinking, feeling, acting and

The Evidence Base

Year	Title	Authors	Methods/Activities	Findings
			Mosaics and virtual Talking Stick Roundtables	engagement -Gives an opportunity for learning about self-other in a community -Empowers students to enact change
2012	Enhancing online student engagement (paper)	Perry, Janzen & Edwards	Photo-cascades, "My" Music Moments, and Word sculptures	-Promotes "student social and academic engagement" (p. 1) -Fosters a sense of being 'real' with each other (student/instructor) -Encourages social engagement -Results in sense of competence (self-confidence and course confidence) -Enhances human connections -Increases sense of community -Facilitates a sense of autonomy -Provides "opportunity for originality and self-expression" (p. 4)
2012	Viewing learning through a new lens: The quantum perspective of learning (paper)	Janzen, Perry & Edwards	QL	-"Educational practice has been outpaced by practice" (p. 712). -QL moves beyond the current "popular" theories (p. 718) -"QLEs take into account humanity and technology... learning takes place ubiquitously" (p. 718)
2012	Engaging students: Strategies for digital natives (paper)	Janzen, Perry & Edwards	Courtroom Scenes, Ethics-opoly, Obituaries, Music, Photovoice	-Involves active doing instead of passive listening -Promotes engagement -Facilitates interactivity between students, teachers, technology and environment -Fosters capacity for inspiration and influence
2013	Quantum learning environments: Making the virtual seem real in the online classroom (book chapter)	Janzen	Haiku-It!, Conceptual Quilting, Collective Quilting, Progressive Poetry, Morning Coffee Forum, Course Climate Checks, Begin with Baroque, Gratitude Letters, Virtual	-Initiates, motivates, sustains and enhances instructor-student and student-student interactions -Contributes to "making online classes real" (p. 134) -Embraces optimal learning multidimentionally -Increases comfort levels -Tangible learning environment -Connects the personal with course/course environment -Evokes emotion -Encourages play—individually and in community

			Talking Sticks, Classroom Eulogies	
2013	Invitational theory: The plus factor (book chapter)	Melrose, Park & Perry	Photovoice, Moment at the Movies, Music, Cartoon Analysis, Reflective poetry, Progressive Poetry, Photostories, Virtual Image-quotes	-Links APTs to concepts -Establishes trust -Makes each other more 'real' in online environment -Maintains and establishes instructor presence -Promotes respect -Stimulates optimism that students can and will succeed -Develops relationships -Allows personalized feedback -Encourages learning in affective domain -Attains a high level of intimacy between student and instructor -Increased engagement

The Present Research: 2014 – 2019

Background

In 2014, we as a research team were awarded another SSHRC Grant (Insight Grant). The research is entitled, *An Exploration of Creative Arts-based Learning Objects in Online, Hybrid and Face-to-face Environments: A Comparison of Engagement, Learning and Quality (Instructional Design)*. This quasi-experimental mixed method, five-year research study focuses on the effectiveness of APTs (learning objects) within different educational milieus. Previous research revealed that APTs are effective in online learning environments. This current study centers primarily on how, and why, APTs work and under what circumstances. Further, this research is designed to also help substantiate and add further insights into the Quantum Perspective of Learning (QL) and the SITE Model that we created earlier (see Chapter 2).

In 2017 Beth (as Principle Investigator) was awarded a Research Incentive Grant from Athabasca University to explore Weblogs as data sources in online nursing and health disciplines. This research focuses on the learning strategy of narrative fiction shared through the medium of Weblogs. In particular, it does seem social media is the "fiction" of our current world. It is not fiction as we once thought of fiction – made up, not real – but rather the "fiction of blogs, tweets, etc., that are in some ways created accounts shared through one lens (the author)". This research seeks to explore how educators can employ a new conceptualization of narrative fiction available in various social media platforms.

The Outputs and Thematic Analysis

This section of the chapter focuses on outputs from 2014-2018 (Janzen, Perry, & Edwards, 2015, 2017; Janzen, MacLean, & Wiebe, 2016; Janzen, Perry, & Edwards, 2017a; 2017b; Janzen, Szabo, & Jakubec, 2016; Perry & Edwards, 2016; Perry, Edwards, & Janzen, 2016; Perry Edwards, & Janzen, 2016; Perry Edwards, & Janzen, 2017; Perry, Edwards, & Janzen, 2018a, 2018b, 2018c; Perry, Janzen, & Edwards, 2014). Thematically, the categories of engagement, enhancement of student needs, creativity, satisfying the quest for 'real,' culture of community, and learning environment remain constant. Additionally, there were additional conclusions regarding the Quantum Perspective of Learning (QL). Therefore, the outputs are explored in terms of conclusions drawn and implications with illustrative examples. Additionally, outputs are presented which have added to, or strengthened, the knowledge base regarding APTs. The outputs are summarized in Table 5.2.

The outputs support what we have found as conclusions/implications in previous studies. These strengthen our conclusions as stated in the previous section of this chapter and as presented in Table 5.1. There have been 15 outputs in the time period from 2014 to 2018. Two of which were invited updated papers (Janzen et al., 2015; 2017), and one which is an invited book chapter in review (Perry et al., 2018c). In the remaining 13 outputs the more salient conclusions are now explored.

Classroom Environment

Many of the conclusions can be seen in terms of the theme classroom environment. These include an increase in knowledge retention, (Perry et al., 2014), and promoting classroom energy (Janzen, Szabo, & Jakubec, 2016). In particular, facilitation of being concise, demonstrating critical thinking, and succinctness has been demonstrated (Janzen et al., 2016).

For example, under the sub theme of being concise, demonstrating critical thinking and succinctness, APT Haiku-it!, is utilized in a second year nursing theory class as a summative teaching tool to promote critical thinking, succinctness and being concise. At the conclusion of the class on the topic of End-of-Life, students are invited to write a Haiku to express what they are going to take away from the lecture. The poems are varied, but challenge the students, and take longer to write than students expect. About half the class hand their poems in for us to review. We receive many types of poems, for example, one written by a young male nursing student which was really powerful and another so heartbreaking from a student who had just lost her best friend in a car accident a month earlier. The following Haiku-It! poems were written to introduce to the students to what a Haiku-It! might look like:

> In the stilled moments
> Of yet darkest night to be
> I will be with you.
>
> I abandon not.
> Even after your last breath
> I am your nurse.

The APTs that use reflection can be focused on the most important concepts within a course (Perry, Edwards, & Janzen, 2016). As mentioned above, Haiku-It! can be used to promote refection. Conceptual or collective quilting can do likewise. Reflective journaling, especially in first year nursing students can make a huge difference as students process what they are learning in a deeper, richer manner (Janzen et al., 2016). An example of this is in reflective journaling.

We find teaching first-year clinical to be an incredible experience. With widened eyes and minds that soak everything up that an instructor says, there is great responsibility for the instructor to develop trust with students. To have students be honest in their journaling is a privilege, not a right. Through their reflective journaling, we get to know the students, and they get to know us more fully in our responses back to them. Not only trust and honesty are developed, but also students' growth and development is enhanced as clinical advances. Journals shared with instructors create a special bond between student and instructor, one which will not be forgotten easily by either person.

Findings also include the ability to link theory to practice. Particularly, APTs help nursing students understand and enact the "art" of nursing (Janzen et al., 2016; Janzen, Perry & Edwards, 2017). In the discipline of nursing there are two components that are taught throughout the curriculum; the science of nursing and the art of nursing. APTs can assist with both components, but it is the affective domain learning outcomes of the art of nursing that can be particularly challenging to teach. It is postulated that to be a good nurse one must possess both components. The science of nursing is taught through the courses which students take. The art of nursing can also be taught through clinical, lab, and theory courses.

Walker (2014) in her dissertation saw the art of nursing as having the following components: "understanding the whole," "focusing on people," "creating meaningful connections," and "just knowing what to do" (pp. 40-66). These components have applicability to Quantum Learning Environments (QLEs) which we believe nursing learning environments can be. The challenge is that the nursing learning milieu also must be patient/client-centered. Walker's components have equal applicability to student-educator/instructor relationships. We have found this particularly through the use of reflective journals, but it can also be seen in the use of Photovoice, photography, art, music, and poetry (Janzen et al., 2016). Corbin (2008) questions whether or not the art of nursing has been lost with technological advances. We emphatically believe that the art of nursing, if lost in an increasingly technological world, can be restored through the use of APTs.

Specifically, APTs can demonstrate the power of acknowledgement (Perry & Edwards, 2016). For example, at one convocation, we had the honor of being on the platform as the very first clinical group that had been taught by one of us. One student in particular gave a big hug as she shook hands with the long line of professors on the stage. She whispered, "Thank you," and then said, "I couldn't have done it without you." Another student exuberantly took a selfie of two of us. These moments are, in many ways, what instructors treasure. Convocation can be a celebration for both students and instructors—a time which is anticipated as a culmination of the nursing education experience. Although for us as educators, convocation is our favorite time of year and we look forward to it immensely, with APTs neither student nor instructor need to wait for acknowledgement until convocation.

APTs acknowledge the impact of students and instructors during a course (Perry & Edwards, 2016). We used APTs in the clinical setting such as Photovoice, poetry, and reflection in the form of reflective journals. Often the APTs are used during clinical post-conferences. These APTs assist in the exchange of two-way feedback which is often poignant—for both student and instructor. The APTs in post-conference give both parties a clear understanding of how each person is feeling about their relationship at a particular moment. APTs give students and learners a chance to communicate about values, views, experiences and feelings in a safe and healthy way. A benefit can be that there are no surprises when it comes to formative or summative evaluations.

Enhancement of Student Needs

As seen through the lens of Malsow's (1954) hierarchy of human needs the outputs from 2014-2018, additional findings are added to those of outputs of 2006-2013. Student needs are further enriched in the areas of human connection, self-competence (both self-confidence and course-confidence), and in the formation of human connections (Janzen et al. 2016a; 2016c; 2016d). Students find their voice through increasing autonomy (Janzen et al., 2016a). APTs can result in inspiration, nurturing, and the empowerment of students (Janzen et al., 2016b) and result in learners gaining a feeling of self-control over the learning environment (Janzen et al., 2017).

Creativity.

The outputs renew support to the theme of creativity in that APTs seem to provide an "opportunity for originality and self-expression" (Janzen et al., 2015, p. 4). The APT enriched learning environment is deemed creative by students (Perry & Edwards, 2016). This can engender excitement in students (Perry et al., 2014). The classroom is deemed "fun" by students when they have an opportunity to participate in APTs (Janzen et al., 2017).

For example, we have previously written about elevator speeches in the section on the outputs from 2006 to 2013. One of the outcomes of the elevator speeches is part of a class devoted to 'Elevator Speech Awards'— akin to the Academy Awards™. The idea of these Elevator Speech Awards is announced in the classes that occur prior to the day students present their speeches, so they are anticipating (and excited about) the awards.

Students play a part in determining who wins the awards. Because the Elevator Speeches are available to them online (before they are presented orally in class) they are asked to review them and anonymously rate each elevator speech from one to five stars online. As their instructors, we tabulate the results and create different categories for the awards. Before award day we buy small trophies, fill them with miniature chocolate bars, and label them with award categories. In addition, each student who wins and award gets a certificate with his or her name on it.

One of the students acts as the Master of Ceremonies for the awards. The student chosen orchestrates the awards and opens the envelopes that contain the names of the winners. The anticipation is palatable as the nominees are read out. Often the students create a hand roll (akin to a drumroll) on their desks as they await the winners. Students who win awards often have pictures of themselves with their awards taken by fellow students.

This APT of elevator speeches is connected to the Elevator Speech Awards. It provides a time for students to have fun and also be recognized by their peers. This creative strategy has continued in our classrooms over several years and has consistently been enjoyed by students and instructor alike.

Satisfying the Quest for Real.

The outputs continue to support the quest for real as students and instructors both experience a sense of being 'real' to each other through the use of APTs (Janzen et al., 2015; Perry & Edwards, 2016; Janzen et al., 2017). This continues to be demonstrated through student-student and student-instructor relationships. The encouragement given to students through social engagement is also another finding supported in the outputs from 2006-2013 (Janzen et al., 2015). Social engagement seems to amplify both the instructors and students' sense of being real.

From Katherine's experience in taking her graduate degree online, she found it initially to be a somewhat lonely time in terms of relationships with other students. Katherine had received her nursing diploma 33 years prior to that and had lived in nursing residence while studying. A sense of community was well-formed in residence as students ate together, learned together, and slept in the same building. Katherine longed for that sense of community in online education hoping that some long-term relationships might be formed.

As Katherine studied online, she engaged as a learner in APTs. APTs that she engaged in did make the other students more real to her than just their postings on the discussion board. More than that, the interactions with instructors and other learners were greatly enhanced when an APTs learning activity was provided. These relationships have endured the test of time as she has moved from graduate student to nursing professor. Although she has seldom met her classmates or instructors in person and communicates with them primarily through email, the relationships developed in online courses are very real to her.

Culture of Community.

The outputs from 2014-2018, continue to show that a culture of community can be a result from utilizing APTs (Janzen et al., 2015; Perry et al., 2016; Perry & Edwards, 2016; Janzen et al., 2017a). Conceptual quilting helps promote a sense of community through the sharing of the quilts in an online quilt gallery (Perry et al., 2014). APTs created for, and utilized in, face-to-face environments such as games and music also increases the sense of community (Janzen et al., 2015).

Two examples illustrate this. In a second-year nursing theory course, one of the concepts taught is ethics. In this course, a Monopoly™-like board game which facilitates a review of ethics and ethical reasoning is a student favorite. The class is divided into groups of 8 players and the game begins. Students develop a sense of community as they talk to each other while playing the game. Anecdotally the students report "having fun" but also learning more about ethics while engaging in the game.

Secondly, music as an APT to help create community. Often popular music is chosen from YouTube™ music videos to illustrate concepts or to stimulate thinking. In the fourth year Leadership class, we show the YouTube™ music video by Rachel Platten (2016) entitled, "Fight Song" at mid-semester when the students are tired and often worn out by the demands of their clinical rotations which have just ended.

Fight Song seems to bring about a sense of community as students collectively express their fatigue and wonder how they are going to get through the rest of the semester. Students realize that they are not alone in their experiences. We encourage the students through this music video and emphasize that they can make it to the end of the semester and that we believe in them both individually and collectively as a class. This seems to give them courage and gives them the strength they need to finish the semester.

One student who was invited back to speak to the second year nursing theory class to give them encouragement talked about the impact that playing this song had on her when she was a fourth year student in her last theory course. We believe that having a former student speak to current students, and playing the music video, had more impact upon the second year students than we could have had.

The Quantum Perspective of Learning.

APTs have lent support to the developing theory of the Quantum Perspective of Learning((QL). "Instructional strategies, especially those within the creative arts, envelop the requirements of quantum learning environments as they encourage holism and holistic development" (Janzen et al., 2017, p. 21). APTs, in terms of the quantum dimensions, encourage holistic learning as the use of multiple APTs can touch the lives of students and their many ways of being in so many aspects in the various quantum dimensions (Janzen et al., 2017).

Weblogs.

The term weblogs were first coined in 1999 by Barger, who was a computer programmer. However, use of the term did not emerge in the literature till 2000 (Ray & Coulture, 2008; Siles, 2011). Since then research related to the use of weblogs and blogging has exploded, particularly related to these as sources of data—especially Big Data (Alsubaie & Madini, 2018; Lee & Bonk, 2016; Piotrowski, 2015; Voivonta & Avraamidou, 2018). Blogging in nursing and related health disciplines, however, is a comparatively new phenomenon (Jones, Garrity, VanderZwan, Epstein, & De La Rocha, 2016; Wilson, Kenny & Dickson-Swift, 2015). There is much to discover about the use of weblogs in nursing education.

> *Social media is the fiction for our times.*
> *(Unknown)*

Weblogs are considered APTs by virtue of their link to creativity and the arts. More especially they are linked to APTs as narrative fiction. "Narrative fiction is the succession of events narrated in [a] verbal, [online or social] medium. The events do not have to be real, they can be taking place in a possible world, but the elements of the narrative have to constitute a coherent whole" (Kiss & Matuska, 2013, para. 4). The use of weblogs in the online learning environment has been shown to enhance social presence, and increases the sense that 'real' people are learning alongside each other (Perry, Edwards, & Janzen, 2018). Further, weblogs facilitate community and can help deliver a positive e-learning environment.

Future Directions

At present we have another year left in our SSHRC study of selected APTs. We are still gathering student and instructor data until December of 2018. We envision three to four publications from this SSHRC study, namely, the instructor perspective, the results of qualitative data, qualitative statistical analysis from the surveys, and a literature review on the current status of creative arts-based teaching strategies (including APTs).

In the funding that Beth has received, there are another two years in this grant to study weblogs and narrative fiction. Data are emerging that links weblogs, as APTs, to previous conclusions. We expect rich, in-depth data as the research proceeds.

The use of weblogs is an area which we will continue to study within nursing and the health disciplines. It seems that weblogs may be a conduit into the future of researching APTs. We believe that weblogs will provide us with fruitful data for future research in nursing education.

Areas for further research also include more in-depth study related to a whole range of APTs. At present we have only focused on a limited number of APTs. Additionally, more research is needed in theory development related to QL and the SITE Model. Narrative fiction and the use of weblogs as a qualitative data collection tool could have great implications for looking at nursing research in unique ways. In Chapter 4 a complete list and explanation of all APTs that were mentioned in Tables 5.1 and 5.2 were presented.

Table 5.2 The Outputs: 2014-2018

	The Outputs: 2014-2018			
Year	Output/Type of Publication	Author	ATP/Focus	Conclusions/Implications
2014	Conceptual quilting: A medium for reflection in online courses (paper)	Perry, Janzen & Edwards	Conceptual Quilting	-Promotes sense of community -Personalizes learning -Fosters self-learning -Increases knowledge retention -Triggers group and personal reflection -Engenders excitement -Facilitates course closure
2015	Engaging students: Strategies for digital natives (paper, updated version)	Janzen, Perry & Edwards	Courtroom Scenes, Ethics-opoly, Obituaries, Music, Photovoice	-Promotes "student social and academic engagement" (p. 1) -Fosters a sense of being 'real' with each other (student/instructor) -Encourages social engagement -Results in sense of competence (self-confidence and course confidence) -Enhances human connections -Increases sense of community -Facilitates a sense of autonomy -Provides "opportunity for originality and self-expression" (p. 4)
2016	Taking the quantum leap: Arts-based learning as a gateway into exploring transitions of senior nursing students (paper)	Janzen, Szabo & Jakubec	Photovoice, Letter Writing, Collective Quilting, Elevator Speeches, Media Collages or Creative Collage	-Inspires, nurtures and empowers students -Letter writing results in "raw honesty" (p. 84) -Promotes trust in instructors -Provides course closure -Encourages meaning-making -Facilitates being concise, critical thinking, and succinctness -Energizes students and instructors -Increases student engagement
2016	Haiku-It! – Reflection in 17 syllables (paper)	Perry, Edwards & Janzen	Haiku-It!	-Focuses reflection on most important concepts -Creates classroom energy -Motivates students
2016	Using online student journaling as an approach to reflection: A creative arts-based strategy (paper)	Janzen, MacLean & Wiebe	Reflective Journaling, Photography, Art, Music, Poetry	-Students willing to take risks -Enrichment of student and instructor's life -Builds confidence -Builds trust -Students gain self-awareness -Ability to link theory to practice -Helps develop the art of nursing in students

2016	Arts-based technologies create community in online courses (book chapter)	Perry & Edwards	Photovoice, Virtual Reflective Centers, Conceptual Quilting	-Encourages engagement -Increases course appeal -Enhances creativity -Develops social cohesiveness -Facilitates sense of community -Provides "safe, structured environment" (p. 184) -Socially motivating through meaningful interaction -Promotes reflection -Furthers interaction with course materials -Acknowledges impact of students/instructors - Makes learning environment creative -Results in social cohesion -Learning consolidation -Environments, students and instructor more 'real' -Potentiates human interactions
2016	Enhancing e-learner engagement by using narrative fiction in online teaching (paper, conference proceedings)	Perry, Edwards & Janzen	Narrative Fiction	- Fictional narrative has positive effects on e-learner engagement - Engagement enhanced by increased interaction, capturing learner attention, and motivating students to participate
2017	Using arts based instructional strategies to engage online learners (paper, conference proceedings)	Perry, Edwards & Janzen	Conceptual quilting, Photovoice, Parallel poetry	- Enhances student-student interaction - Deepening of rapport -Advanced innovation/creativity and risk taking -Personalization of the learning environment
2017	Building blocks: Enmeshing technology and creativity with artistic pedagogical technologies (paper)	Janzen, Perry & Edwards	Parallel poetry, Photovoice, Conceptual Quilting	-Develops community -Enhances creativity -Allows for risk-taking -Students/instructors become 'real' to one another -Increased sense of collegiality -Allows students to have fun -Promotes "sense of control over learning environment" (p. 12) for students and instructors -Fosters mutual respect -Engagement is an outcome -Enables art of discipline to emerge instead of solely science of discipline -APTs provide low cost technologies

2017	Engaging students: Strategies for digital natives (paper, updated version)	Janzen, Perry & Edwards	Courtroom Scenes, Ethics-opoly, Obituaries, Music, Photovoice	-As above
2017	Use of weblogs as data sources in qualitative educational research in distance education (poster, conference proceedings)	Perry, Edwards & Janzen	Weblogs	-Effective method for obtaining data from geographically dispersed participants in qualitative studies
2018	Using arts based instructional strategies to engage online learners (paper, conference proceedings)	Perry, Edwards & Janzen	Photovoice, Photo-cascade, Poetry	-Engagement leads to increased motivation and learner achievement
2018	Use of weblogs as data sources in qualitative research sources exploring e-learning topics (paper under review)	Perry, Edwards & Janzen	Weblogs	- Advantages include research participants can be from anywhere, reduced participant fatigue, potentially reaches vulnerable, socially isolated, and study participants from the non-dominant culture - Barriers and precautions include need to assess credibility of blogger, avoiding commercial weblogs, amount of potential data overwhelming, need for a process for sifting through data to locate relevant content
2018	Enhancing e-learner engagement by using narrative fiction in online nursing and health disciplines courses (book chapter, invited)	Perry, Edwards & Janzen	Narrative Fiction	-Enhances social presence -Increases sense of 'real' people learning alongside each other -Facilitates community -Positive e-learning environment
2018	Revisiting the seven definitive questions: A further exploration of	Janzen, Perry & Edwards	The Quantum Perspective of Learning	-Envelope the prerequisites of quantum learning environments (QLEs) -Allow for holism and holistic development

	the quantum perspective of learning (paper under review)			
2018	Enhancing e-learner engagement by using narrative fiction in online teaching (poster, conference proceedings)	Perry, Edwards & Janzen	Narrative fiction	-Positive effects on engagement -Enhances interaction - Captures learner attention -Motivates Participation -Social media emerges as a type of narrative fiction which has importance in online course design/teaching -Source of context of human experience -Human stories have power to help students to act, react or think about beliefs/values -Reduces transactional distance -Enhances learning

Conclusion

We have endeavored to leave no aspect of APTs covered in terms of who, what, where, how, and why APTs work. There have been many 'aha' moments. We have learned a great deal about APTs from our research in the analysis of the data and through the development of subsequent papers which have been written and published. It has been an incredible journey that has not yet ended. The best is yet to come.

References

Alexander, E. M. (2015). Physical and digital disengagement behaviours in the university classroom. *Electronic Thesis and Dissertation Repository*. 2759. Retrieved from https://ir.lib.uwo.ca/etd/2759

Alsubaie, A., & Madini, A. A. (2018). The effect of using blogs to enhance the writing skill of English language learners at a Saudi University. *Global Journal of Educational Studies, 4*(1), 13-31.

Arum, R., & Roksa, J. (2011). *Academically adrift: Limited learning on college campuses*. Chicago, IL: University of Chicago Press.

Benson, S. G., & Dundis, S. P. (2003). Understanding and motivating health care employees: Integrating Maslow's hierarchy of needs, training and technology. *Journal of Management, 11*(5), 315-320.

Block M. (2011) Maslow's hierarchy of needs. In: Goldstein S., & J.S. Naglieri (Eds.) *Encyclopedia of child behavior and development*. Boston, MA: Springer.

Chipchase, L., Davidson, M., Blackstock, F., Bye, R., Colthier, P., Krupp, N. & Williams, M. (2017). Conceptualising and measuring student disengagement in higher education: A synthesis of the literature. *International Journal of Higher Education, 6*(2), 31-42.

Corbin, J. (2008). Is caring a lost art in nursing? *Nursing Studies 45*(2), 163-165. Retrieved from http://www.journalofnursingstudies.com/article/S0020-7489(07)002313/fulltext

Cote, J. E., & Allahar, A. L. (2007). Ivory tower blues: A university system in crisis. Toronto, Canada: University of Toronto Press.

Cox, A. M., & Marris, L. (2011). Introducing elevator speeches into the curriculum. *Journal of Education for Library and Information Science, 52*(2), 133-141. Retrieved from http://www.jstor.org/stable/41308888

Cummings, E.E. (1954/1994). 100 selected poems. New York: Grove Press. Retrieved from https://hellopoetry.com/poem/1674/a-wind-has-blown-the-rain-away-and-blown/

Demir, S., Demir, S. G., Bulut, H., & Hisar, F. (2014). Effect of mentoring program on ways of coping with stress and locus of control for nursing students. *Asian Nursing Research, 8*(4), 254-260.

D'Souza, J. F., Adams, C. K., & Fuss, B. (2015). A pilot study of self-actualization activity measurement. *Journal of the Indian Academy of Applied Psychology, 41*(3), 28-33.

Edwards, M., Perry, B., Janzen, K., & Menzies, C. (2012). Using the artistic pedagogical technology of photovoice to promote interaction in the online post-secondary classroom: The students' perspective. *Special Conference Issue of the Electronic Journal of e-Learning, 10*(1), 32-43.

Garrison, D. R. (2016). *E-learning in the 21st century: A community of inquiry framework for research and practice.* New York: Taylor & Francis.

Gorski, P. C. (2015). Equity literacy for all. *Educational Leadership, 7*(26), 72-40.

Gorski, P. (2016). Rethinking the role of "culture" in educational equity: From cultural competence to equity literacy. *Multicultural Perspectives, 18*(4), 221-226.

Gorski, P. C., & Swalwell, K. (2015). Equity literacy for all. *Educational Leadership, 72*(6), 34–40.

Henrie, C. R. (2016). *Measuring student engagement in technology-mediated learning environments.* Proquest Dissertation 10134118. Brigham Young University.

Henrie, C. R., Halverson, L. R., & Graham, C. R. (2015). Measuring student engagement in technology-mediated learning: A review. *Computers & Education, 90*, 36-53.

Ilies, R., Wagner, D., Wilson, K., Ceja, L., Johnson, M., DeRue, S., & Ilgen, D. (2017). Flow at work and basic psychological needs: Effects on well-being. *Applied Psychology, 66*(1), 3-24.

Jack, K. (2017). The meaning of compassion fatigue to student nurses: an interpretive phenomenological study. *Journal of Compassionate Health Care, 4*(1), 2-8.

James, K. (2016). Barriers to treatment and the connection to Maslow's hierarchy of needs. *Counselor Education Capstone, 18,* 1-35. Retrieved from http://digitalcommons.brockport.edu/edc_capstone/18

Janzen, K.J. (2013). Quantum learning environments: Making the virtual seem real in the online classroom. In S. Melrose, C. Park, & B. Perry (Eds.)

Teaching health professionals online: Frameworks and strategies. Edmonton, AB: AU Press.

Janzen, K.J., MacLean, H, & Wiebe, M.A. (2016). Using online student journaling as an approach to reflection: A creative arts-based strategy. In A. Peterkin & P. Brett-MacLean (Eds.). *Keeping reflection fresh: Top educators share their innovations in health professional education.* (pp. 344-347). Kent, OH: Kent State Press.

Janzen, K., Perry, B., & Edwards, M. (2011a). Becoming real: Using the artistic pedagogical technology of Photovoice as a medium to becoming real to one another in the online environment. *International Journal of Nursing Education Scholarship, 8*(1), 1-17.

Janzen, K., Perry, B., & Edwards, M. (2011b). Aligning quantum learning with instructional design: Exploring the seven definitive questions. *International Review of Research in Open and Distributed Learning, 20*(7), 1-18. Retrieved from https://files.eric.ed.gov/fulltext/EJ963980.pdf

Janzen, K., Perry, B., & Edwards, M. (2012a). A classroom of one is a community of learners: Paradox, artistic pedagogical technologies, and the invitational online classroom. *Journal of Invitational Theory and Practice, 17,* 28-36.

Janzen, K., Perry, B., & Edwards, M. (2012b). The entangled web: Quantum learning, Quantum learning environments and Web technology. *Ubiquitous learning: An international journal, 4*(2), 1-16. Retrieved from http://ijq.cgpublisher.com/product/pub.186/prod.173

Janzen, K.J., Perry, B., & Edwards, M. (2012c). Engaging students: Strategies for digital natives. *Academic Exchange Quarterly, 16*(3), 116-123.

Janzen, K.J., Perry, B., & Edwards, M. (2012d). Viewing learning through a new lens: The quantum perspective of learning. *Creative Education, 3*(6), 712-720.

Janzen, K.J. (2013). Quantum learning environments: Making the virtual seem real in the online classroom. In S. Melrose, Park, C., & Perry, B (Eds.) *Teaching health professionals online: Frameworks and strategies.* Edmonton, AB: AU Press.

Janzen, K.J,, Perry, B., & Edwards, M. (2015a). Engaging students: Strategies for digital natives, *Academic Exchange Quarterly, 19*(4) (republished). Retrieved from http://rapidintellect.com/AEQweb/win2015.htm

Janzen, K.J., Perry, B., & Edwards, M. (2015b). *Engaging students: Strategies for digital natives.* SIB STEM Education, 105-113. Retrieved from http://www.rapidintellect.com/AE/8si-stem.htm.

Janzen, K. J., Perry, B., & Edwards, M. (2017a). Building blocks: Enmeshing technology and creativity with artistic pedagogical technologies. *Turkish Online Journal of Distance Education, 18*(1), 4-21.

Janzen, K.J., Perry, B., & Edwards, M. (2017b). (Updated) Engaging students: Strategies fordigital natives. STEM SOTL, XIV, 1-9. Retrieved from http://www.rapidintellect.com/AE/8si-3-volume-14.htm

Janzen, K.J., Szabo, J., & Jakubec, S.L. (2016). Taking the quantum leap: Arts-based learning as a gateway into exploring transitions for senior nursing students. *Journal of the Canadian Association for Curriculum Studies, 14,* 77-91.

Jones, K., Garrity, M. K., VanderZwan, K. J., Epstein, I., & De La Rocha, A. B. (2016). To blog or not to blog: What do nursing faculty think? *Journal of Nursing Education, 55*(12), 683-689.

Kiss, A., & Matuska, A. (2013). Narrative Fiction. In *Introduction to the study of cultures and literatures in English*. Szeged, Hungary: Universitas Scientarium Szegediensis. Retrieved from http://www.jgypk.hu/mentorhalo/tananyag/introduction/6_narrative_fiction.html

Kuh, G. D. (1999). How are we doing? Tracking the quality of the undergraduate experience, 1960s to present. *The Review of Higher Education, 22*(2), 99-120.

Kuh, G. D., Schuh, J. H., & White, E. J. (1991). *Involving colleges: Successful approaches to fostering student learning and personal development outside the classroom*. San Francisco: Jossey-Bass.

Lee, J., & Bonk, C. J. (2016). Social network analysis of peer relationships and online interactions in a blended class using blogs. *The Internet and Higher Education, 28*, 35-44.

Main, E. (2004). Student Disengagement in Higher Education: Two trends in technology. *Journal of Educational Media & Library Sciences, 41*(3), 337-349.

Maslow, A. (1954). *Motivation and personality*. New York: Harper & Row.

Maslow, A. (1964). *Religions, values, and peak experiences*. Harmondsworth, England: Penguin Books.

Maslow, A. (1968). *Toward a psychology of being*. (2nd ed.) New York: Van Norstrand Reinhold.

McLeod, S. (2007/2013). Maslow's hierarchy of needs. *Simply Psychology*, 1-8. Retrieved from http://www.simplypsychology.org.malsow.html

Melrose, S., Park, C., & Perry, B. (Eds.). (2013). *Teaching health professionals online: Frameworks and strategies*. Edmonton, AB: AU Press. Retrieved from http://www.aupress.ca/index.php/books/120234

Michalos, A. C. (2017). Education, happiness and wellbeing. In *Connecting the Quality of Life Theory to Health, Well-being and Education* (pp. 277-299). Cham, Switzerland: Springer.

Perry, B. (2006). Using photographic images as an interactive online teaching strategy. *The Internet and Higher Education, 9*(3), 229-240.

Perry, B. (2009). *More moments in time: Images of exemplary nursing*. Edmonton, Canada: AU Press.

Perry, B., & Edwards, M. (2009a). Strategies for creating virtual learning communities. In *Nursing and Clinical Informatics: Socio- Technical Approaches*, B. Staudinger, V. Hob, H. Ostermann, (Eds.). (pp.175-197). Hersey, CA: IGI Global.

Perry, B., & Edwards, M. (2009b). *Creating a culture of community in online courses*. Retrieved from https://auspace.athabascau.ca/handle/2149/2159

Perry, B., & Edwards, M. (2010a). Creating a culture of community in the online classroom using artistic pedagogical technologies. *Using Emerging Technologies in Distance Education*. In G. Veletsianos (Ed.).

Edmonton, AB: AU Press. Retrieved from http://www.veletsianos.com/2010/11/14/data-on-our-open-access-book/

Perry, B., & Edwards, M. (2010b). Interactive teaching technologies that facilitate the development of online learning communities in nursing and health studies. *Teacher Education Quarterly*, 147-273. Retrieved from http://teqjournal.org/perry_edwards.html

Perry, B., & Edwards, M. (2012). Creating an "invitational classroom" in the online educational milieu. *The American Journal of Health Sciences, 3*(1), 7-16. Retrieved from http://journals.cluteonline.com/.

Perry, B., & Edwards, M. (2016). Creating a culture of community in the online classroom using artistic pedagogical technologies. In G. Veletsianos (Ed.). *Emerging technologies in distance education*. Edmonton, AB: AU Press. Retrieved from http://www.aupress.ca/index.php/books/120258

Perry, B., Edwards, M., & Menzies, C. (2012). Using the artistic pedagogical technology of photovoice to stimulate interaction in the online post-secondary classroom: The teachers' perspective. *Ubiquitous Learning: An International Journal, 3*(3), 117-128.

Perry, B., Dalton, J., & Edwards, M. (2009b). Photographic images as an interactive online teaching technology: Creating online communities. *International Journal of Teaching and Learning in Higher Education, 20*(2), 106-115.

Perry, B., Edwards, M., & Janzen K.J. (2016). *Using arts based instructional strategies to engage online learners*. EdMedia 2016: World Conference on Educational Media and Technology, Vancouver, Canada, June 27, 2016.

Perry, B., Edwards, M., & Janzen K. (2017). *Enhancing e-learner engagement by using narrative fiction in online teaching*. Proceedings from the European Conference on E-Learning. Porto, Portugal, October 26-27, 2017.

Perry, B., Edwards, M., & Janzen, K. (2018a). Use of weblogs as data sources in qualitative research exploring e-learning topics. *The Electronic Journal of e-Leaning*. (in review)

Perry, B., Edwards, M., & Janzen, K. (2018b). Enhancing e-learner engagement by using narrative fiction in online nursing and health disciplines courses. C. Jarvis & P. Gouthro (Eds.), (invited book chapter, in review)

Perry, B., Janzen, K., & Edwards, M. (2011). Creating invitational online learning environments using learning interventions founded in the arts. *eLearning Papers, 27*, 1-4. Retrieved from http//www.elearningpapers.eu

Perry, B., Janzen, K., & Edwards, M. (2012). Creating invitational online learning environments using learning interventions founded in the arts. *Opening Learning Horizons*. Retrieved from http://elearningpapers.eu/en/elearning_papers

Perry, B., Janzen, K., & Edwards, M. (2012c). Enhancing online student engagement. *eLearning Papers, 30*, 1-5.

Perry, B., Janzen, K., & Edwards, M. (2014). Conceptual quilting: A medium for reflection in online courses. *E-learning papers, 36*, p. 1-4.

Perry, B., Janzen, K., & Edwards, M. (2016). Haiku it! Reflection in 17 words. In A. Peterkin & P. Brett-MacLean (Eds.). *Keeping reflection fresh: Top educators share their innovations in health professional education.* (pp. 33-36) Kent, OH: Kent State Press.

Piotrowski, C. (2015). Emerging research on social media use in education: A study of dissertations. *Research in Higher Education Journal, 27,* 1-12.

Platten, R. (2016) Fight song. [Music video]. Retrieved from https://www.youtube.com/watch?v=xo1VInw-SKc

Ray, B.B., & Coulter, G.A. (2008). Reflective practices among language arts teachers: The use of weblogs. *Contemporary Issues in Technology and Teacher Education, 8*(1), 6-26.

Shernoff, D. J., Csikszentmihalyi, M., Schneider, B., & Shernoff, E. S. (2014). Student engagement in high school classrooms from the perspective of flow theory. In *Applications of flow in human development and education* (pp. 475-494). Netherlands: Springer.

Simons, J. A., Irwin, D. B., & Drinnien, B. A. (1987). *Maslow's hierarchy of needs.* New York: West Publishing Company.

Souter, A.K., O'Steen, B., & Gilmore, A. (2014). The student well-being model: A conceptual framework for the development of student well-being indicators. *International Journal of Adolescence and Youth, 19*(4), 496-520.

Siles, I. (2011). From online filter to web format: Articulating materiality and meaning in the early history of blogs. *Social Studies of Science, 41,* 737–758.

Van Eck, R. (2006). *Digital game-based learning: "It's not just the digital natives that are restless..." EDUCAUSE, 41*(2), 16-30

Voivonta, T., & Avraamidou, L. (2018). Facebook: a potentially valuable educational tool? *Educational Media International, 54*(4), 1-15.

Walker, R. (2014). *The art of nursing in public health.* [Thesis] Retrieved from https://dt.athabascau.ca/jspui/bitstream/10791/49/3/The%20Art%20of%20Nursing%20in%20Public%20Health.pdf

Wang, C., & Burris, M. A. (1997). Photovoice: Concept, methodology, and use for participatory needs assessment. *Health education & behavior, 24*(3), 369-387.

Washor, E., & Mojkowski, C. (2014). Student disengagement: It's deeper than you think. *Phi Delta Kappan, 95*(8), 8-10.

Watson, C. (2014). *The rest of the story: Paul Harvey, conservative talk radio pioneer.* Retrieved from https://www.npr.org/2014/10/09/354718833/the-rest-of-the-story-paulharvey-conservative-talk-radio-pioneer

Wilson, E., Kenny, A., & Dickson-Swift, V. (2015). Using blogs as a qualitative health research tool: A scoping review. *International Journal of Qualitative Methods, 14*(5), 1-12

Chapter 6

Trying Something New: Motivating Educators to Give APTs a Try

If you have even an ounce of creativity, and are willing to take a risk, then give APTs a try! Our aim in this chapter is to motivate you to use APTs (either the ones we have developed or APTs you design) to add some spice to the learning activities you offer your students. To begin the etymology of the word motivation is explored followed by a discussion of the applicability of motivation theory to APTs. Next is a discussion of why APTs are well suited to education and a review of some of the qualities educators who use APTs need to have. A quick review of how APTs help create an invitational learning milieu is provided. Finally, we describe how we are sharing the concepts of APTs with others through conferences and publications. If you could use a strategy or resource that is completely free but that has many potential positive benefits for learners (and for you) would you take a chance and try it? That is our invitation to you. Try APTs.

Motivation Theory

The word motivation comes from the Medieval Latin meaning to move or impel, and further is found within the word motivate, meaning having will or drive (Online Etymology, 2018). Thus, to motivate, or to have motivation, can be seen as both a verb and a noun. As a verb motivate is an action word. As a noun motivate can be seen as a word that denotes being acted upon.

As human beings, to perform or do anything we must have a degree of motivation. That motivation can be either intrinsic or extrinsic in nature (Reiss, 2012). Motivation can be intrinsic in that the forces that propel us into action come from within. If we are extrinsically motivated the reasons we do things come largely from external forces. Motivation is essential for humans to move forward or even to sustain existence. Motivation is the impetus for us to strive for goals and to act (Ryan & Deci, 2000). Such goals include the goal of achieving a degree in an educational pursuit and activities that help students reach this goal (Ross, Perkins & Bodey, 2016; Vanllerand et al., 1993).

Lazowski and Hulleman's (2016) meta-analysis, while not exhaustive, identifies almost 1500 studies that center on motivation and motivational theories. There are many motivational theories that help explain why APTs are effective. While it is beyond the scope of this book to explore all the pertinent theories in detail, some motivation theories are reviewed and a discussion of how they apply to education and APTs is included in the following sections.

Cognitive Dissonance Theory

When cognitive dissonance (Festinger, 1962) happens, there is a competition in our minds between two conflicting ideas. A certain level of tension results, especially when the conflicting beliefs are quite divergent. Cognitive dissonance motivates us to act or change something so that the dissonance is resolved, and the discomfort caused by trying to hold two conflicting ideas is diminished.

APTs such as minute at the movies (where the students' long-held values are challenged by a character or story-line portrayed in a movie) can induce dissonance and motivate learners to act (including the changing of a long-held value). Attitudinal change in nurse learners is often a sought-after learning outcome that is a challenge to attain through conventional learning activities. APTs can be effective techniques to help learners achieve affective domain outcomes such as awareness, attending, cherishing, and many others.

Endowed Progress Effect

According to the endowed progress effect, "when people feel they have made some progress towards a goal, they will feel more committed towards its achievement. Conversely, people who are making little or no progress are more likely to give up early in the process" (Conti, 2015, para. 13). Applying this theory to APTs, it is apparent that one of the benefits of these activities is that there are no right or wrong answers and that everyone who participates succeeds. In other words, everyone who engages in an APT is making progress toward a goal (of learning). As the depth of discussion triggered by an APT deepens, and learning becomes more meaningful, learners build upon these little successes and work toward progressive learning.

Photovoice is a perfect example. When the instructor shares a digital image, and asks a reflection question, all responses are correct. All students feel successful. Some answers to reflection questions will be more insightful than others (although all answers are considered equally right). These more insightful responses may generate further class discussion on a topic thus deepening the learning for all.

Expectancy-value Theory

Expectancy-value theory (Eccles & Wigfield, 2002) takes the premise that students take on tasks that have value to them and believe that success is possible—therefore possessing self-belief. APTs have value, and students believe that they can succeed due to the nature of APTs (no incorrect responses). APTs are full of challenging moments where students dig deep for the answers. While APTs seem deceptively simple at the onset, APTs can require considerable thought and a degree of effort from participants.

The contribution of expectancy-value theory can be especially seen in the APT of Haiku-It! Students are asked to consolidate an entire one hour lecture into three lines of a haiku. This action requires determination, struggle, distillation, priority-setting, and analysis from the learner. The result is Haiku-It poems that are beautiful and that display evidence of learning and understanding.

Interest Theory

Interest theory (Hidi & Renninger, 2006) suggests that interest in an activity motivates pursuit of that activity. APTs are interesting for students. Interest is felt to motivate engagement (Harackiewicz, Tibbets, Canning & Hyde, 2017). APTs take everyday common activities and present them to students. Often these activities involve simple actions, such as the use of felt pens and paper to create quilt-blocks for conceptual quilting. APTs call upon students to create. For example, word sculptures invite students to create their own unique sculpture made of words. No two word sculptures are alike in terms of emphasis, content, color, or shape. Word sculptures motivate students in that this APT is not difficult to do. Value can be found for students in that students are told that the purpose of doing the world sculpture to is review concepts that stood out for them during a lecture. Surprisingly, students place great value on their creations. This will be discussed later in the chapter, but students value APTs and exude a sense of pride in their work. The individual feedback that is given by the teacher to the students about their APTs also aids in creating value for APT activities.

APTs and Education

APTs are well suited to education. Just as in the Quantum Perspective of "Learning (QL), [the] learning environments [in education] are living systems that grow, evolve, and develop through the passage of time and space. ... Learning environments are dynamic spaces that support the needs of learners, instructors, and educational systems" (Janzen, 2011, p. 65). From the very first day in a course, the stage is set for learners' growth and development as professionals. Students and teachers can look forward to all that can be as the learners successfully complete their program of studies. The course, as it develops and evolves with APTs, allows that growth and development. APTs, while they can be entertaining and fun for learners, always have a purpose. Many APTs can be used for the purpose of review and to generate reflection. As previously mentioned, Word Sculptures can be utilized as a form of lecture review. Courtroom Scenes can also be used for a review of salient concepts. Other forms of APTs such as PD Sculptures are used to give shape and understanding to more complex concepts such as burnout.

Educators have the freedom to shape lectures, and teachers are able to choose to infuse creativity within those lectures. APTs provide a vehicle to provide creativity. This is accomplished by choosing one or more APTs a lecture and then by enthusiastically introducing them to students. It can take a little time for students to become eager participants in APTs, but if the educator is excited about the value of these activities, and a few early adopters in the class do them, the remainder of the group will soon be equally enthusiastic and anticipate the next opportunity to do an APT.

Qualities Educators Have That Use APTs

This chapter would not be complete if we did not also review some of the qualities educators who use APTs need to have. One of the primary qualities that educators need to start with is that of curiosity. As you are reading this book, you've got curiosity! The second is a desire to try something new in the classroom. The third is to have courage.

"Courage is not the absence of fear but rather the judgement that something is more important than fear. The brave may not live forever but the cautious do not live at all" (Cabot, 2010, para 1.) To truly live as an educator one must constantly be taking chances. This is the fourth attribute. To phrase "taking chances" in terms of APTs, an educator acknowledges the feelings of "What if it doesn't work?" and thinks instead, "What if it does work? What difference will that make for me and my students?" We each have faced moments of nervousness as we tried APTs. Repeatedly we have found that APTs work with our students! This has been reinforced many times during the past 13 years of research.

The fifth attribute is that of enthusiasm. Enthusiasm is contagious. If you are enthusiastic about the value of APTs then students are willing to try APTs. When students see enthusiasm demonstrated by the teacher this energy is reflected back in terms of participation, effort, and degree of satisfaction that students feel.

Finally, intentionality is a key attribute educators require to use APTs successfully in nursing education. You need to choose an APT carefully so that it matches the desired learning outcome. Using APTs successfully is not achieved by simply sprinkling these "fun" learning techniques into your lectures. There is an intentional process required as educators choose the right APT to help learners meet the learning outcome desired.

The Teacher and APTs

For us, teaching young people to become compassionate, competent nurses is among the more privileged of all careers. Educators have the opportunity to share their knowledge and experience and directly impact the professional and personal lives of their students and indirectly impact the lives of the patients and families these students will care for upon graduation. There are few professions where you have such potential to make a difference for so many other people.

As educators, we all have reasons why we chose to teach. For some of you, over time, some of the reasons may have become embers. For others, the flame is still burning brightly. Whether you are an ember or a flame, for those of you who are looking for a way to stoke the fire, APTs provide much fuel for imagination and creativity. As learners become more excited about learning, there may be positive outcomes for you too.

We believe that passion drives educators to be the best they can be. A passionate educator is constantly looking for ways to deliver educational material in new and different ways. APTs offer an avenue to do just that. With a repertoire of 35 APTs, and myriads of ways that APTs can be adapted, the classroom continues to be a space/place where students and teachers can look forward to learning. In essence, APTs can rejuvenate educational material.

Educational content in part, reflects the teacher's attitudes, thoughts, and feelings about that material. Even for the most committed and passionate of teachers, the educational material can stymie the teacher. For example, teaching theory courses can be considered to be "dry" by some students.

How can a teacher make "dry" material come alive? We believe that APTs can help. For example, we have had feedback from students that the content of theory classes is enlivened with the use of APTs. Some theory students even said that the classes became "enjoyable. With APTs students can begin to look forward to each lecture as they progressively try out various APTs through the semester. Students also report that they begin to wonder "What do we *get* to do today?" rather than "What do we *have* to do today?" APT infused classrooms become places of wonder.

As a beginning point, do an informal self-evaluation of your own classrooms. What attributes do you desire most in your classroom experience? Do you believe that the learning experience you offer learners could be improved? Do you want more energy, excitement, interest, and successful learning in your classrooms?

The use of APTs becomes the process that can be followed to help rejuvenate the classroom experience. Table 6.1 represents a body of research on APTs. (Chapter 4 gives more examples). For example, do you want to have more of a shared sense of community among students in your classes? If it is community you want, try drama. Do you want more engagement in your classroom? If it is engagement you aim for, try Word Sculptures or Minute at the Movies. Do you want to create a greater sense of being 'real' to your online learners? To help give that sense that there is a live and engaged instructor leading the online class, try Photovoice or Photostory. Do you want your students to experience creativity or to have opportunities to be creative? To generate creativity, try Conceptual Quilting or Haiki-It!

Table 6.1 Desired Outcomes and APTs

	Targeted Outcome and APTs That Can Be Utilized
Student Engagement	Photovoice, Virtual Reflective Centers, Conceptual Quilting, The Great Debate, Point-Counterpoint Debates/Reflection, Drama (role playing and Courtroom Scenes), Movie Analysis, Theme Songs, Story-telling, Story-writing, Parallel Poetry, Photocascades, "My Music Moments, Word Sculptures, Courtroom Scenes, Ethics-opoly, Obituaries, Music, Letter Writing, Elevator Speeches, Media Collages, Creative Collage
Creation of Community	Photovoice, Conceptual Quilting, Point-Counterpoint Debates, Drama (role playing and Courtroom Scenes), Movie Analysis, Theme Songs, Story-telling, Story-writing, Parallel Poetry
Manifestation of Being "Real"	Photovoice, Virtual Reflective Centers, Conceptual Quilting, Moment at the Movies, Cartoon Analysis, Reflective Poetry, Progressive Poetry, Photostories, Virtual Image Quotes, Narrative Fiction
Course Engagement	Photovoice, Letter Writing, Elevator Speeches, Media Collages, Creative Collage
Enhanced Learning Environment	Photovoice, Reflective Journaling, Photography, Music, Poetry
Creativity	Photovoice, Virtual Reflective Centers, Conceptual Quilting, The Great Debate, Point-Counterpoint Reflection
Course Closure	Photovoice, Virtual Reflective Centers, Conceptual Quilting, The Great Debate, Point-Counterpoint Debates/Reflection, Collective Quilting, Classroom Eulogies, Letter Writing, Elevator Speeches, Media Collages, Creative Collage
Safe Learning Environment	Photovoice, Virtual Reflective Centers, Conceptual Quilting, The Great Debate, Point-Counterpoint Reflection
Interactivity/Interaction	Photovoice, Virtual Reflective Centers, Conceptual Quilting, The Great Debate, Point-Counterpoint Reflection, Drama (role playing and Courtroom Scenes), Movie Analysis, Theme Songs, Story-telling, Story-writing, Parallel Poetry, Photocascades, "My Music Moments,

	Word Sculptures, Courtroom Scenes, Ethics-opoly, Obituaries, Music, Haiku-It!, Collective Quilting, Progressive Poetry, Morning Coffee Forum, Course Climate Checks, Begin with Baroque, Gratitude Letters, Virtual Talking Sticks, Classroom Eulogies
Intimacy/Meaningful Connections/Develops Relationships	Photovoice, Virtual Reflective Centers, Conceptual Quilting, The Great Debate, Point-Counterpoint Reflection
Community Development	Virtual Reflective Centers, Conceptual Quilting, Photovoice, Parallel Poetry, Narrative Fiction
Motivation	Virtual Reflective Centers, Conceptual Quilting, Photovoice, Haiku-It!, Narrative Fiction
Self-disclosure/Authentic Interactions	Reflective Poetry, Minute at the Movies, Our Community Soap Scenes, Theme Songs; Reflective Journaling, Photography, Art, Music, Poetry
Spontaneous Play	Photovoice, Haiku-It!, Collective Quilting, Progressive Poetry, Morning Coffee Forum, Course Climate Checks, Begin with Baroque, Gratitude Letters, Virtual Talking Sticks, Classroom Eulogies
Foster Wellbeing and Confidence	Photovoice, Haiku-It!, Letter Writing, Elevator Speeches, Media Collages, Creative Collage
Find Personal Voice	Photovoice, Haiku-It!, Creative Collage, Elevator Speeches
Further Application of Course Content	Photovoice, Parallel Poetry, Conceptual Quilting, Letter Writing, Elevator Speeches, Media Collages, Creative Collage

Students and APTs

Basically, it is like the leadership dancing video (Sivers, n.d.) – you, as an educator, need some early adopters and a critical mass of participants to get full engagement in an APT. Then the other slower adopters become willing to take a risk and participate. When students see their peers taking a risk and engaging in APTs it is almost contagious. The enthusiasm passes from the early adopters to other students. While there may be some slower adopters, they too eventually join in and participate.

We think that this has never been so evident as in comments and actions from students. We demonstrate this with two examples. While both examples are of outcomes, the second example is also of process.

We include Classroom Temperature Checks mid-way in each semester. On one such Temperature Check, additional questions were utilized. Particularly one question was, "What do you want more of?" One of the more surprising replies was, "More coloring!" This spoke to us of the impact that a simple act of coloring had on these students.

In this next example, during a lecture on the end of life, we utilized, D'Errico's (2013) "a room, a hat, and panic button" (p. 120). In this drawing/coloring activity, students are invited to draw a room where they would like to spend their last hours of life. The students then draw hats to represent the people that would surround them. Finally, they draw a panic button which represents what it would be that would cause them to push that panic button. Students then are invited to share their drawings with the class and explain them. A class discussion ensues.

D'Errico's activity remains an effectual example of early, mid, and late adopters. Some students take up this activity immediately and others, as mid adopters, then join in. In one case, there was one student who took considerable time to decide to engage. When he did, he thoughtfully produced one of the most intriguing and poignant pictures in the entire class. This reinforced to us that late adopters can get as much out of an activity as early adopters—sometimes more.

In online and blended environments APTs are invitational in nature and can be built into the course curriculum. Students in graduate online or blended course are particularly excited about using APTs. This excitement carries on as students showcase their work to their instructor and fellow students. APTs bring a sense of being 'real' to each other, and the sense that the teacher is 'real' as well. In an online course, one may never move beyond "seeing" their teacher other than by the words he/she types onto a computer screen. APTs have the potential to create this sense of being 'real' to one another, in part because APTs infuse humanity into classrooms.

This showcasing of student work can also occur in face-to-face learning environments. In Katherine's personal office there is an open-door policy—students can drop by anytime, as long as the door is open students know they are welcome to come in and talk. On the wall adjacent to the desk there is a bulletin board which is filled with various examples of student APTs. There are Haiku-It! poems, drawings, and Photovoice offerings. Katherine finds it to be especially gratifying when students ask to put their APT on the bulletin board in the classroom and then come to the office and see their work displayed there too.

As well, in face-to-face learning environments, APTs are written into lesson plans (see Chapter 7 for selected lesson plans using APTs). In the six years we have been using APTs in the face-to-face classroom, not one student has refused to give APTs a try. For example, at the conclusion a capstone leadership class one student wrote and expressed her appreciation for the many ways that APTs had been used to help her engage in reflection. The student felt that it had helped her prepare for being a new graduate nurse.

Spreading the Word

One question we often ask ourselves is how to get educators to use APTs? We believe that it starts with the teacher – being enthusiastic about the idea of the APT and having confidence others will enjoy it and learn from APTs is key. When we think of the pillars of invitational theory (Purkey, 1992), we also believe these traits in the teacher are key to the success of an APT.

Invitational theory, pioneered by William Purkey (1992), suggests that there are five pillars of invitational theory (central values). The invitational theory values that correspond with APTs are optimism and intentionality. Optimism suggests that one's worldview is based upon a belief in positive outcomes. Just as in the Quantum Perspective of Learning (QL) (Janzen, 2013), Purkey emphasizes that human beings have infinite potential.

Intentionality refers to a deliberate creation of learning environments by teachers who possess respect, trust, and care (Purkey, 1992). It is with these values of optimism and intentionality that environments become serendipitously invitational (Melrose, Park & Perry, 2013). If a teacher is intentional about using APTs in the classroom, the students are likely to try APTs as well.

The teacher must be daring in a way – and be willing to fail - but have the confidence that he/she will not fail with the strategy. There is a braveness and excitement that is contagious (students think if the teacher thinks this is a good idea maybe I will try). For example, when Katherine first started using APTs in the face-to-face learning environment, she was at the beginning of her career as an academic and preparing for her first theory course. The key point is that she believed in APTs, and that APTs had the power to reach students in a new and exciting way. She remembers her first classroom experience as necessitating bravery and excitement on her part. It took courage for her to even try and use APTs in a learning institution that frequently utilized conservative Power Point™ presentations as the main strategy in lectures.

After Katherine introduced herself to the class, she explained the premises of APTs and that students would be invited to use APTs throughout the semester. The first APT she used was Photovoice. When that APT was successful with students, she tried Courtroom Scenes in her second lecture.

Before her first class using APTs she was walking down the long hallways to another building on campus, she was excited but terrified. No one that she knew in the faculty had used such an unconventional teaching strategy. In the end, the students loved the APTs and she received feedback from students that they found the Courtroom Scenes were not only fun but informative. Walking back to her office that day, she felt confident in following-up Courtroom Scenes with Ethic-opoly in her next class. She felt a sense of joy that Courtroom Scenes had gone so well. This sense of joy led to her using APTs consistently in all the classes that semester. The student evaluations at the end of term revealed that APTs really struck a chord with students. The students' excitement fed Katherine's excitement about these techniques and has manifested itself in the creation of additional new APTs suitable for the face-to-face learning environment.

If you become as APT believer, how can you inspire other teachers you work with to try this approach? It comes down to the education of teachers. Your enthusiasm goes a very long way to helping others try APTs. For example, Katherine and Margaret attended a conference in Portugal, and following the conference, Katherine was invited to present APTs as a teaching strategy to her home nursing faculty. This presentation at home caused quite a stir with faculty. One faculty member was overheard saying, "Damn, now I am going to have to change the way I teach!" This brought a smile to the faces of all in attendance!

After the presentation Katherine was asked by her faculty members if she could teach them how to use APTs. In response to this request, with the help of the Nursing Education Scholar, a learning community was organized surrounding the Quantum Perspective of Learning (QL) and APTs. This learning community was held once a month. Later, at a university-wide retreat, the learning community jointly presented their experiences to other faculty—spreading the word university wide. As a result, another presentation was given to the university community through the Academic Development Centre on QL/APTs.

Educating others about the outcomes of using the APTs is another way of increasing the use of APTs in the classroom. We remember one excited professor who met us in the hallway who exclaimed, "They work! They really work!" and proceeded to explain the APT she had tried in her classroom that day.

Research that is published or shared at conferences gets others to use APTs. We presented at a conference in Lethbridge, Alberta about QL/APTs. After the presentation, one professor told us, "This one presentation made it worth coming to the conference for me." When other educators get excited about using APTs the potential of these teaching strategies is magnified.

In an interesting twist, research about Photovoice and Conceptual Quilting done by other scholars we are not connected with is now being presented at conferences we attend. It is like a domino effect --- we started something that is now used, adapted, and studied by many other educators in nursing and other disciplines.

Conclusion

In this chapter, motivation has been explored, as well as APTs which can trigger motivation. A discussion on teachers and APTs, and students and APTs, was presented to help readers familiarize themselves with qualities needed to use APTs successfully. Invitational Theory (Purkey, 1992) was touched upon in terms of APTs. The Chapter concluded with a brief discussion on how to encourage others to use APTs.

"Success in the . . . classroom is, to a large part, accounted for by the teachers' engagement with technologies" (Zhou & Teo, 2017, p. 26). It is the teachers' attitudes and enthusiasm that begins the motivation process for student learning. To a large degree, "students exist symbiotically in the classroom with the teacher" (p. 27). With APTs both student and teacher can benefit in very real ways. This is rewarding both for the teacher and for the student. In the next Chapter (7) several lesson plans are provided that utilize APTs at different points of the lecture.

References

Cabot, M. (2010) *Goodreads*. Retrieved from https://www.goodreads.com/quotes/572007-courage-is-not-the-absence-of-fear-but-rather-the

Conti, G. (2015). *Eight motivation theories and their implications for the classroom*. Retrieved from https://gianfrancoconti.wordpress.com/2015/07/27/eight-motivational-theories-and-their-implications-for-the-foreign-language-classroom/

D'Errico, E. M. (2013). Teaching facilitation of patient choice at the end of life. *Journal of Nursing Education, 52*(2), 120-120.

Eccles, J.S., & Wigfield, A. (2002). Motivational beliefs, values and goals. *Annual Review of Psychology 53*, 109-132.

Festinger, L. (1962). *A theory of cognitive dissonance* (Vol. 2). Redwood City, CA: Stanford University Press.

Harackiewicz, J. M., Tibbetts, Y., Canning, E., & Hyde, J. S. (2014). Harnessing values to promote motivation in education. *Advances in motivation and achievement: A research annual, 18*, 71–105. http://doi.org/10.1108/S0749-742320140000018002

Hidi, S., & Renninger, K. (2006). The four-phase model of interest development. *Educational Psychologist, 41,* 111-147.

Janzen, K.J., Perry, B., & Edwards, M. (2011). Aligning the quantum perspective of learning to Instructional design: Exploring the seven definitive questions. *International Review of Research in Open and Distance Learning, 12*(7), 56-73. Retrieved from http://www.irrodl.org/index.php/irrodl

Janzen, K.J. (2013). Quantum learning environments: Making the virtual seem real in the online classroom. In S. Melrose, C. Park, & B. Perry (Eds.). *Teaching health professionals online: Frameworks and strategies.* Edmonton, AB: AU Press.

Lazowski, R. A., & Hulleman, C. S. (2016). Motivation interventions in education: A meta-analytic review. *Review of Educational Research, 86*(2), 602-640.

Melrose, S., Park, C., & Perry, B. (2013). *Teaching health professionals online: Frameworks and strategies.* Edmonton, AB: AU Press.

Online Etymology Dictionary (2018). *Motivate.* Retrieved from https://www.etymonline.com/search?q=motive

Purkey, W. W. (1992). An introduction to invitational theory. *Journal of Invitational Theory and Practice, 1,* 5-15.

Reiss, S. (2012). Intrinsic and extrinsic motivation. *Teaching of Psychology, 39*(2), 152-156.

Ross, M., Perkins, H., & Bodey, K. (2016). Academic motivation and information literacy self-efficacy: The importance of a simple desire to know. *Library & information science research, 38*(1), 2-9.

Ryan, R. M., & Deci, E. L. (2000). Intrinsic and extrinsic motivations: Classic definitions and new directions. *Contemporary educational psychology, 25*(1), 54-67.

Sivers, D. (n.d.) First follower: Leadership lessons from dancing guy-- YouTube. Retrieved from https://www.google.ca/search?source=hp&ei=X5PTWuDfKeuYjwSf6oaI Dg&q=leadersh ip+dancing+video&oq=leadership+dancing+video&gs_l=psy0.12634.24.2 1.0.3.3.0.195.3230.0j19.19.0....0...1c.1.64.psy-ab..2.22.3335...0i131k1j0i22i110i30k1.0.RHnfAUU_KO4

Vallerand, R. J., Pelletier, L. G., Blais, M. R., Briere, N. M., Senecal, C., & Vallieres, E. F. (1992). The Academic Motivation Scale: A measure of intrinsic, extrinsic, and amotivation in education. *Educational and psychological measurement, 52*(4), 1003-1017.

Zhou, M., & Teo, T. (2017). Exploring student voice in teachers' motivation to use ICT in higher education: Qualitative evidence from a developing country. *International Journal of Educational Technology, 4*(1), 26-3

Chapter 7

Selected Lesson Plans

Lesson Plan Example 1

    Lesson Plan Lecture 1 N 2XXX
    INTRODUCTION AND CONCEPTS

1. Introduction to N2111 including expectations and evaluative activities (55 min)
   a. NAME CARDS and INTRODUCTIONS (25 min)
      i. If you could be any cartoon character, who would you be and why? (20 min—5 min prep and 15 minutes response)
      ii. Learner's Role: Q: "In order to make this learning opportunity best for me, what would I like to see my classmates do?" (5 min) students' obligations and responsibilities (whiteboard & recorder)
      iii. Negotiable and non-negotiable areas (break, laptops, cell phones/texting)
      iv. Instructor's Role: Q: "In order to make this learning opportunity the best for me, what would I like to see the instructor do? (5 min) role of instructor (white board & recorder)
   b. SYLLABUS (5 min)
   c. COURSE OUTLINE (5 min)
   d. ASSIGNMENTS (10 min)
      i. HHE Paper (5 min)
         1. RUBRIC
         2. 30% Hardcopy due at beginning of class Jan 28th
      ii. IN CLASS INDIVIDUAL ASSIGNMENTS (20%) Quiz—Multiple Choice/Short Answer....Helps prepare for final exam... 4 assignments 5% each. Must be present in class to do these or have a Dr.'s note. Not returned to students but can come to discuss with me
      iii. FINAL EXAM

                1. 25%, Somewhere in between April 15-25 set by Registrar's Office
                2. Multiple Choice/Short Answer questions
                    a. Content-based on all required reading, lectures, student presentations and instructor concept presentations
            e. GROUPS for PRESENTATIONS (5 min) Groups of 5 students each. Picking a concept—all have to be different. Instructor Concept Presentation
                i. 5% for initial proposal; 20% for group presentation mark TOTAL 25%
2. **Creative arts-based teaching strategies/ APTs (5 min)**
    a. **Photovoice introduced in 1214 reflective journaling/Haiku/Poetry/Minute at the Movies/ games/drama/role play/debates/Word Sculptures. One or two APTs each week.**
3. BREAK 15 min
4. Discuss School of Nursing framework in relation to foreground/background of the concepts as they occur in practice (5min) Discussion/PPT
5. Review DOH's (5 min) Quiz: List all (13). Who got all 13? More than 10? In clinical what were the most visible DOH's? Least visible? Why?
6. THE CONCEPT OF HEALTH (15 min) Individual experiences of health
    a. Prep (5 min)
    b. Class discussion (5-10 min)
7. Presentation on Concepts (45 min)
    a. Etymology of word concept (3 min)
    b. Exploration of what a concept is (5 min)
        i. Question... define the word concept (3min)
        ii. Sextant and uses (5 min)
            1. GPS Systems
            2. Longitude and Latitude
        iii. Individual experience
        iv. How are concepts constructed? (2 min)
            1. Comparison: What are the similarities?
            2. Reflection: What are the differences?
            3. Abstraction: What is the concept that arises from this? Or what meaning do I now ascribe to what I have learned?
        v. Tree Exercise (10 min]

             1. Write down similarities and differences as you can. If you were to pick one concept that you could use to describe these images what would it be?
          vi. Q: Are there any generic concepts? GENERALIZATION (2 min)
              1. i.e. HOPE
       c. Concept or Condition (10 min)
           i. Groups of 2 or 3—discuss whether word is a condition or a concept or both and why
          ii. APT: Photovoice...
8. COLLECT NAME CARDS (5 min)
9. OUTLINE FOR NEXT WEEK (5 min)
    a. CONCEPTS AND NARRATIVES
    b. Essential that students attend this class as HHE paper is based on the guest speaker's presentation
    c. Half class on concepts, primary health care strategies, health promotion with a focus on application to experience of health collaborative partnership model
    d. Half class presentation by a patient regarding human health experience
    e. APT next week: Word Sculptures

Lesson Plan for End of Life

1. Introduction
2. Death & Dying (Video 8 min) https://www.nytimes.com/2013/01/11/us/fatally-ill-and-making-herself-the-lesson.html
    a. Kubler-Ross (1969) statement (2 min)
    b. Awareness (Strauss & Glazer) 4 kinds (2 min) http://groundedtheoryreview.com/2015/12/19/awareness-of-dying-remains-relevant-after-fifty-years/
    c. Truth Telling (5 min)
  Story of Mother-in-law/Bowel Ca What would you have done? The rest of the **story**....
    d. Denial (2 min)
        i. Define
       ii. Is it ever helpful?
    e. Hospice (2 min)
        i. Die at home? Die in hospital? Why?
       ii. What is holistic care?
    f. Role as a Nurse (10 min)

- YouTube video (7 min) **Minute at the Movies** (Avnet (1992) Fried Green Tomatoes [film] Universal Studios.)iAVn9CKw
    1. What was Idgy's role?
    2. What was Sipsy's role?
    3. What do you think your most important role is/will be?
  g. Teach supportive Care Model (3 min) http://www.virtualhospice.ca/Assets/HPC%20Nursing%20Standards_20081127165937.pdf
  h. Betty Davis YouTube video (4 min) http://www.virtualhospice.ca/en_US/Main+Site+Navigation/Home/Support/Support/The+Gallery/For+Professionals/Betty+Davies+_+Supportive+Care+Model_+Six+dimensions+of+nursing.aspx
  i. Palliative Care (2 min)
  j. **Mid Semester Class Temperature Check** (5 minutes)
  k. BREAK TIME 20 min
3. Part 2—120 min
  a. Obituaries
     i. **YouTube video Say Something** (4 min) Great Big World (2014) https://www.youtube.com/watch?v=-2U0Ivkn2Ds
     ii. 92 years old, look back on your life, what would you want to say? Write own **obituary**—2 paragraphs (15 min)
     iii. What do you want to be remembered for?
     iv. What do you think patients want to be remembered for?
     v. How can you assist your patients make sense of their lives? Their deaths?
  b. Greatest Fears (5 min)
     i. A room, a hat and a panic button (15 min drawing time + 10 min small group discussion + 20 min report—clarify major findings)
     ii. Our desires and fears about death and dying are not that much different than other people
     iii. What patients fear most?
     iv. How can we help patients to come to terms with their fears?
  c. There is nothing more that we can do. (10 min)
     i. Story of Mr. T.M.
     ii. **Poem** Balm of Gilead

       iii. What do you think you could do when others turn away and give up or keep trying the same interventions with no success?
   d. Palliative Sedation (5 min)
       i. 2 kinds: analgesics (Morphine) and anxiolytics (Midazolam)
       ii. Case Study: Mrs. M. Codeine ATC
       iii. What would you do?
   e. Death Vigils (5 min)
       i. Dying alone Case Study: Mrs. L.
       ii. What is your role?
   f. After death care (10 min)
       i. What kinds of things happen in after death care?
       ii. Story: Ms. M. Last act of service
   g. Haiku-it! (15 min)
   h. Next week:
       i. Papers due Friday
       ii. Legal Issues
       iii. Send group topics
- In Closing: YouTube video Ben Breedlove (8 min) https://www.youtube.com/watch?v=MlaQK3LyWC8

Selected Lesson Plan 3

N4XXX Summer 2015 Week 7 Lecture
1. Introduction & Overview of Today's Class (3 min)
2. Db Rubric Evaluations—due at 1600 today via dropbox (1 min)
3. Major Paper Expectations (5 min)
4. Debrief about Clinical (5-10 minutes)
   Elevator Awards from Elevator Speeches (30 min)

       Part 1 **Letter writing Activity** (45 min)

BREAK (20 min) (10am roughly)
Chinese symbols for change (5 min)
    In what way is change dangerous? In what ways is it an opportunity?
    Also involves being inevitable + discomfort. How many of you like change?
Transitions. Always involve going from old life to new life. One is known and one is not known.
Rites of passage. How many rites of passage can you name? (3 min)

How is graduating from MRU a rite of passage? (Into the world of nursing)

Describe your first day in clinical. How did you feel? Did you sleep the night before? (5 min)

First 3 months most stressful... Normal to have anxiety

How many of you still don't sleep the night before clinical?

6-12 Months adjustment period

My research study (5 min)

Hierarchy of Needs.... who can tell me about this model by Abraham Maslow? (2 min) (Reading Text).

Fulfillment on the job (5 min)

A grad nurse's hierarchy of needs.... Go through each level with students (5 min)

Model of Success in Quality Work Environments (1 min) (reading)

Predictability the 5 W's of the environment. (1 min)

What makes a QWE consistent, stable and familiar? (Think to your last clinical experiences) part of it is the environment but a lot of it is the people you work with)

Buddies vs. preceptors vs. mentors. (2 min)

What do you think people expect of you as a GN? What do you expect of yourself? How can you accept the limitations as a new practitioner? (5 Min discussion)

Small steps win the race. **Story** of tortoise and hare (have someone tell the story/moral of the story) (3 min)

Metaphor for being a new grad... construction in Calgary. Story of when I was a second-year student and working in the hospital. Story of when I was a new grad (5 min). (45 min to here)

Q. What strategies can you use to help manage the change from being an SN4 to GN? (Discussion) (5 min)

5 Strategies (multiple slides) Text. (3 minutes)

Tips (1 min)

Journaling (5 min) How many people journal? What benefits do you find in journaling? Challenge to keep a journal. My experience of keeping a journal/ writing.

Top 8 tips for first year of transition. (1 min)

How can Maslow's hierarchy of needs help me prioritize my care? (Discussion 5 min)

Object lesson: water (large bottle vs. small bottle) (1 min)

Exercise: organizing a typical day (10 min) Did you set times aside to take breaks? Go to the bathroom?

Selected Lesson Plans 135

    Reading: ... turning off the switch (2 min)
    Delegation metaphor: Reading (3 min)
    Violence and workplace bullying
        Quote (1 min)
        What examples of bullying have you seen in clinical? (5 min)
    What advice would you give someone who is being bullied?
    10 ways to address bullying (2 min)
    Crucial conversation skills (3 min) Story about new grad being bullied (IF TIME)
    Oh the places you'll go... Quote + BN = generalist (1 min)
        Know a lot about a lot of things.

    Part 2... **Letter writing activity** (45 minutes)

Selected Lesson Plan 4

    N4XXX Week 8 Lesson Plan

1. Overview
2. **YouTube video** (20 min) **TED Talk**—Think of this in terms of yourself being a leader in nursing. Why do you do what you do? Have you ever thought about it?
3. I have a dream **YouTube video** 5:18 min—
https://www.youtube.com/watch?v=MlaQK3LyWC8
Each of you have a dream inside you, something you want to do in your life, and something that you passionately care about. Dreams in nursing and often life begin with mission and vision statements. These statements can help you figure out what path you want to follow.
4. YouTube video 5 min on mission statements... think of this in terms of you instead of a company
5. YouTube video Leadership Vision Statements (5 min)
6. How many of you have your own vision/mission statements? Today after a few more slides we are going to spend some time crafting our own mission and vision statements.
7. **Share story of my journey to being an educator.**
8. My mission statement
9. My vision statement—wrote the first statement in 2002. Revised it again for this class.

10. What things in your life support you and sustain you? Pair share
11. What is your 5-year plan? Brainstorm as a class
    a. Marriage, children, pay off loans, graduate education in nursing or not, NP, get a permanent job, be casual and travel
    b. Look at what is on blackboard for links…
    c. What may actually happen may look more like this…complexity (ping pong)
12. Write your own mission/vision statements. Handout (30 min)
13. Resumes, Cover letters & Thank you notes
    a. Blackboard resources
    b. 15 minutes to have a look at those who brought their examples to share and then in the larger group discuss questions and common themes discovered
    c. We will quickly breeze through the tips and ah-has…focus on overall suggestions that come to mind as a group.
14. What is the difference between a resume and a curriculum vitae? (2 slides)
15. Key tips
16. What are your options when things suck and you feel stuck?
    a. Leave → get a new job → feels good for a while → same issues creep in → leave and find another job or consider what you are doing to be complicit in what is happening
    b. Stay → nothing changes (new people come and go, new organizational ideas come and go → leave or stay rooted and get progressively disenfranchised by the system and people)
    c. Stay → question what is happening at the person-person level and how that translates to or gets influenced at, the bigger picture level → get involved in committees and associations and get involved in change.
    d. Change theory: Kramer (1968) investigated the dimensions of role socialization in novice nurses and reasons for the early abandonment of the profession.
    e. How do we translate our individual perceptions to the reality of the bigger picture and share the burden of difficulty? When we keep leaving and reporting on the fact that things aren't good, we also have to take accountability of our complicity in the situation. The new manager will also want to know why you left and what you did to contribute to influencing the needed change your way. Leaving and bringing the "cloud" with you will not be welcomed. So be thoughtful of what you include in your exit interviews and in how you speak of our former

place/culture of employment...framing and language is everything.
17. Health literacy
    a. What questions do we have to ask ourselves when we read this statement?
    b. What is this statement saying to you?
    c. How will you continue learning and supporting nursing as a discipline and profession as you move forward in your career?
    d. What counts – continuing education, certification, being involved in workplace committees, journal clubs, challenging "relic" practices with research, becoming a researcher in your practice setting, reading the *Canadian Nurse* and *Alberta RN, Pediatric Nursing, OR Nursing, Oncology, Palliative Care Nursing,* etc.
18. Anti-intellectualism
    a. Qualifiable (What is nursing?)
    b. Risk of loss of identity → building educational capacity → influences quality of care
    c. Students and professors aren't finding time to read...what are the implications?
    d. How we read – technology changing our ways of communicating, obtaining and using information.
19. Transfer –shift away from unidirectional research utilization and evidence-based practice EBP models (Cochrane randomized trials)
    a. Moves from one party to another to develop or improve products, services or practices
    b. Gap between the generation of evidence and uptake in practice
    c. Who needs to be in the loop: practitioners, policy makers, researchers, administrators
    d. Similar to the theory/practice gap or discipline/professional gap → research/practice
    e. Need organizational support (uptake in Cancer Agency, Kidney Foundation, Diabetes Society, etc.)
    f. Translation:
        i. Data analysis, collection, synthesis → developing and implementing initiatives, teaching and action plans, sharing findings in "real time" (nursing rounds, journal clubs, etc.), transforming practice → more research questions and inquiry

20. Evidence informed
    a. WHO
        i. Evidence-informed health policy-making is an approach to policy decisions that aims to ensure that decision making is well-informed by the best available research evidence. It is characterized by the systematic and transparent access to, and appraisal of, evidence as an input into the policy-making process.
    b. Stages in the process
        i. DEFINE: Clearly define the health problem or issue
        ii. SEARCH: Efficiently search for research evidence
        iii. APPRAISE: Critically and efficiently appraise the research sources
        iv. SYNTHESIZE: Interpret/ form options or recommendations for practice or policy based on the literature found
        v. ADAPT: Adapt the information to a local context
        vi. IMPLEMENT: Decide whether to implement the adapted evidence into practice or policy
        vii. EVALUATE: Evaluate the effectiveness of implementation efforts
    c. The Canadian Nurses Association defines *evidence-informed decision-making* as "a continuous interactive process involving the explicit, conscientious and judicious consideration of the best available evidence to provide care" (Canadian Nurses Association [CNA], 2010, p. 1).
    d. Evidence-informed practice means ensuring that health practice is guided by the best research and information available.
        i. Good evidence identifies the potential benefits, harms, and costs of an intervention.
        ii. Evidence may be of a qualitative or quantitative nature.
        iii. In the health promotion context evidence can come from sources including; population health statistics, scientific journals and publications, evaluation reports, and locally collected data.
    e. Ciliska - http://www.nccmt.ca/pubs/2008_07_IntroEIPH_compendium ENG.pdf

Selected Lesson Plans 139

      i. Define – clearly define the question/problem
      ii. Search – efficiently search for research evidence
      iii. Appraise – critically and efficiently appraise the research sources
      iv. Synthesize – interpret/form recommendations for practice based on the literature found
      v. Adapt - the information to a local context
      vi. Implement – decide whether (and plan how) to implement the adapted evidence into practice or policy
      vii. Evaluate
      viii. Knowledge Translation
      ix. Knowledge Transfer (CIHR)
21. What are some of the trends in healthcare? (aging population/technology)
22. Genomics: How would RNs get involved in this topical area? Nursing education, policy, administration, clinical practice
23. Environmental issues impacting health
    a. Role of Health Canada:
      i. Committed to making the population of Canada among the healthiest in the world
      ii. Ensures that human health is included as a component of environmental assessment
      iii. Environmental assessment is a planning tool that provides decision makers with the information they need to approve projects that are compatible with a healthy and sustainable environment
      iv. The federal government of Canada (2004) instituted indicators (measuring sticks) designed to provide information for environmental sustainability and health and well-being as well as for economic growth and lifestyle choices of Canadians. The indicators are:
          1. Air quality
          2. Greenhouse gas emissions
          3. Freshwater quality
24. How does environmental health impact nurses? Video Idle no More 11:40 min
25. Aging Population, ageism. Who can define this?
    a. Ageism, a prevalent, socially constructed way of thinking about and behaving toward the elderly. The effects of ageism lead steadily toward discrimination and

marginalization of elderly people (Lowell, 2006; McPherson & Wister, 2008).

26. Trends and Issues in Canada
    a. Student Presentation: Aboriginal Health and Healing (5-10 min)
    b. What mental health challenges impact nursing? Canadians"?
    c. National Expert commission (2012) (2 slides)
    d. Stats
        i. In 2014 1/3 of homeless population
        ii. 2014 5.8 million > 65 yrs old
        iii. 215 billion spent on health care in 2015 (estimated 2.1% increase + 4.5 billion/year)
        iv. 2012 – 268,500 RNs in Canada 2014—293,205 RNs in Canada.
            1. 15% growth in RN/NPs 50% growth of LPNs
27. Career Possibilities
    a. Brainstorm the areas that students have heard you can work
        i. RA, camp, prison, parish, government, legal or curriculum consultant (medication errors/charting/legal counsel…malpractice lawsuits- CARNA)
28. A day in the life of an academic educator
    a. Do your professors have CARNA memberships? How are they classified?
    b. How did you find yourself in this position? Remembering my story of coming to this line of work on the first day of class…it wasn't all STOP signs along the way. It was about opportunities to influence change. Being just above the comfort line.
29. How do you get there? Prezi presentation (5 min)
30. Why graduate school?
    a. How has educational preparation changed over the years…
    b. In 2005, undergraduates were speaking the same language of epistemology, ontology and methodology…literature reviews and writing for publication and presentations at conferences are common practices for many nursing students…culture of shifting expectations (Canadian Nursing Students' Association)…how would you prepare your paper for publication – journals that accept student work— *Academic Exchange Quarterly*, Athabasca University
    c. Do I choose a nursing MN or other – What are the options affiliated with nursing?
    d. Journals:

Selected Lesson Plans 141

> *Policy and Practice...Social Policy & Practice, Public Policy*
> *(Government)*
> *Education*
> *Interdisciplinary Studies*
> *Public Health*
> *Nursing Philosophy/Research*

  e. Let's say I want to move to a particular province (spouse) – Check the website, who works there...if I have the freedom, I may just move where I choose.
  f. Do I have to work to pay for school – distance versus face-face...accessibility of libraries (agreements) and between institutions for your committee...funding!!!!!
  Who has the money and reputation...competitive.

31. **My journey through grad school**
32. Revolution in Nursing Research:
    Important sites to find links to the research questions and what is being funded...funding does matter to institutions of higher learning and your track record in terms of who you choose to work with (network/connections) as you move forward in your career.
33. Advanced Nursing Practice: Nurse Practitioners: NPs Assigned a restricted permit indicating the stream(s) of practice
    3 years of practice recommended...preferably in the area that you want to make your focus/specialty
    Requirements:
    a. Hold a master's degree, normally in nursing.
    b. Have a minimum grade point average (GPA) of 3.0 in the master's degree, or 3.0 on the last 20 half-course equivalents in the baccalaureate degree if applying to the MN/NP program;
    c. Have a minimum of 3 years full-time clinical practice (4,500 hours) in the area appropriate to the proposed Nurse Practitioner (NP) focus.
    d. Have successfully completed one graduate level half-course equivalent to University of Calgary Nursing 661; one equivalent to Nursing 663; and one equivalent to Nursing 665;
    e. Provide a reference from a person in authority who can attest to current clinical competence and suitability for the NP.
    History, physical exams, ordering diagnostic tests, prescribing physical therapy – some require Master's degree preparation
34. **Debate** (25-30 min)
    a. Afterward read section from the *Globe* and *Mail* (new slide)

35. Brainstorm for afternoon session.... what questions would you ask of career professionals in different domains of practice?
36. **Photovoice** (30 min) Hand in by Wednesday evening typed 1 ½ - 2 pages with image. Can use own mage. Image has to be non-recognizable people/not students/ Creative Commons/Flickr.
Last thing before you go... get into your Db groups and decide how you will divide up the readings for next week. You will each share a reading in a 5-minute sum up (refer to **Water Cooler Talks**).

Conclusion

We have travelled a journey together over the past seven chapters. Now the journey has come full circle (Eliot, 1969); where our paths have crossed for a time we have been fellow travellers. But in our travels, we have changed as information has been presented and new ideas put forth. Information and ideas we may not have considered before.

Being an educator is a challenge. Perhaps one of the greatest challenges is that of change. All around us are forces of change (Melrose, Park & Perry, 2013). While change keeps us from being stagnant and directionless, it can also provide a sense of bewilderment. In education, change can seem constant. Change, however, doesn't have to be negative (Fullan, 2001).

Change can also lend itself to the positive. Enter the use of APTs. You have learned through reading these pages, an exciting new way of engaging your students. Through the creative arts students are able to take risks, experience increasing self-actualization, and develop an increasing sense of community. In a very real way, students become "co-creators" (Stevens & Nies, 2018, p.32) with their teachers. Most of all, students are able to have fun!

Through the choices we give students in our lectures, APTs become a creative arts-based teaching strategies that meet student where they are at. Students grow and develop as they reflect upon what they are learning and on their practice. Through this students become more reflective beings who are then more humane. The opportunities that are given through the use of APTs also allow students to become real—oh, so much more than a student identification number! Conversely, educators become real as well. Through this realness, we meet in the middle—educators through the delivery of APTs including feedback, and students through their raw honesty. What is simply left over is simply the "wow" factor.

We as educators have grown as a result of using APTs in our classrooms. From the feedback on student evaluations of instruction, students express their growth and development as well. The end product is a world where educators and students meet with respect and amiability. In reality, APTs create a win-win situation.

We urge you to give APTs a try! APTs really are magical in many ways. May you begin journeys of your own with APTs. We know they will be full of excitement as you walk a path that will be inspiring to you—and your students.

References

Eliot, T. S. (1969). *The complete poems and plays of TS Eliot. London,* Faber.

Fullan, M. (2001). *The new meaning of educational change.* Routledge.

Melrose, S., Park, C., & Perry, B. (Eds.). *Teaching health professionals online: Frameworks and strategies* (pp. 129–154). Edmonton, AB: Athabasca University Press.

Stevens, K. P., & Nies, M. A. (2018). Transforming nursing education in a 140-character world. The efficacy of becoming social. *Journal of Professional Nursing, 34(1), 31-34*

Index

A

APTs (artistic pedagogical technologies), ix, 1, 3, 23, 31, 118
    effectiveness of, 9
art of nursing, 100
assumptions, 15

B

Begin with Baroque, 68
big T technology, 34
Bloom's revised taxonomy, 31
building blocks of learning, 18

C

choices., ix
Class Temperature Checks, 68
classroom environment, 99
closure, 81
Cognitive Dissonance Theory, 116
Collective Quilting, 51, 90
community, 4
Community of Inquiry Model, 21
Conceptual quilting, 50
connected, 27
connectivism, 5
constructivism, 5
Courtroom Scenes, 66
creative play, 35
creativity, ix, 40, 41, 86, 102, 115
cues and conduits, 22
culture of community, 103

D

David Bohm, 14
digital native, 32, 77
Disengagement, 76

E

early adopters, 123
educational objectives, ix
educational technologies, 75
edutainment, 32, 35
E-Journaling, 73
Elevator Speeches, 70
Endowed Progress Effect, 116
engagement, 122
Enhancement of Student Needs, 101
entanglement, 12, 13
Entropy, 23
Ethics-opoly, 67
Expectancy-value Theory, 117
external locus of control, 79

F

feedback, 25
five assumptions, 9
flow, 77
free play, 41
frontal brain, 36

G

grants, 75
Gratitude Letters, 69

H

Haiku-It!, 59, 99

hard technology, 43
humanity, 3

I

innovative, 25
Intelligence, 18
Interest Theory, 117
invitational theory, 124

L

learning activities, 1
learning environment, 90
Letter Writing, 71
little t technology, 34
living environments, 20

M

Maslow, 78
Media Collage, 72
Meeting of Student Needs, 78
Minute at the Movies, 59
Miss Frizzle, 42
Mission Impossible, 54
Morning Coffee Forum, 67
motivation, 115
music, 104
My Music Moments, 65

N

Narrative fiction, 72
Narrative weblog, 73

O

Obituaries/Music, 67
online theatre, 63
Our Community Soap Scenes, 60

P

Parallel Poetry, 57
PD sculptures, 65
Photo Cascades, 64
Photostories, 69

Photovoice, 49
play, 35, 37, 87
Poetic Learning, 55
poetry, 3
principles, 15

Q

qualities of nurse educators, 118
quanta, 16
quantum, 11, 16
quantum communication, 14
quantum dimensions, 16
quantum mechanics, 11, 12
Quantum Perspective of Learning (QL), 4, 5, 9, 20, 21, 99, 104, 118
quantum physics, 11
Quote Share, 70

R

real, 88, 103
real and authentic medium, 4
realms of knowledge, 17
reflective journaling, 100
research, 9
risk-taking, 39

S

safety, 79
salon, 10
self-actualization, 83
self-transcendence, 84
SITE Model, 20, 21, 34
soft technology, 43
stoke the fire, 119
story writing, 61
story-telling, 61
student engagement, 76
superposition, 12, 13

T

technology, 19, 21, 32
tech-savvy, ix
The Great Debate, 53
The SITE Model, 4

Theme songs, 60
theoretical foundation, 11
theory-practice gap, 43
trust, 26

U

universalistic, 19

V

Virtual Reflective Centers, 53
Virtual Talking Stick Roundtables, 63

W

waves and particles, 12
weblogs, 104
wellbeing and confidence, 81
Word Sculptures, 62